THE MONSTER
GOD

THE MONSTER
GOD

Coming *to* Terms
with the Dark Side *of* Divinity

JOHN R. MABRY

At the height of the heavens,
the angels, whose voice I hear, glorify me.
I am beneath the sun, a wandering ant,
small and black, a rolling stone
reaches me,
crushes me,
dead,
in the sky
the sun blazes furiously,
it blinds,
I cry out:
"it will not dare"
it dares.
—George Battille, *Inner Experience*

The Apocryphile Press
1700 Shattuck Ave #81, Berkeley, CA 94709
www.apocryphile.org

© Copyright 2008 by John R. Mabry. Originally published in
2008 by O Books, an imprint of John Hunt Publishing, Ltd.
Apocryphile edition, 2015.

Printed in the United States of America
ISBN 9781940671840

Table of Contents

This book is dedicated to

DR. MARGARET DANA

who encouraged me
to exorcise the Monster God.

I fled Him, down the nights and down the days'
I fled Him, down the arches of the years;
I fled Him, down the labrinthine ways
Of my own mind; and in the mist of tears
I hid from Him, and under running laughter.
Up vitaed hopes I sped;
And shot, precipitated,
Adown Titanic glooms of chasmed fears,
From those strong Feet that followed, followed after
But with unhurrying chase,
And unperturbéd pace,
Deliberate speed, majestic instancy,
They beat—and a Voice beat
More instant than the Feet—
"All things betray thee, who betrayest Me."

Francis Thompson
"The Hound of Heaven"

Introduction

Hunted by the
Hound of Heaven

I have always had the feeling that I was fundamentally
irredeemable. I remember vividly as a child of six or seven
being ushered into the pastor's office by my mother. I was
sure that I was going to Hell. I didn't know how I knew it, but I
was terrified—and quite certain—of it. The pastor of our mid-
sized Southern Baptist Church led me through some scripture
verses, assuring me that God would not let me slip through his
fingers no matter what happened. I appreciated Pastor Jones'
patient and concerned explanations. But even as I was walking
back out to where my mother was waiting I knew he was wrong.
God was out to get me. I knew it.

Nevertheless, I did everything I was supposed to do to win
God's favor. The stories of God's wrath poured out upon the
heathen nations in the Old Testament were there for my sole
benefit, a foreshadowing of what was in store for me. The many
sermons I endured vividly depicting the horrors of Hell made me
faint with panic at what would most assuredly be my final resting
place. As a child I remember crying myself to sleep, wondering if
my mother would endure Hell on my behalf. I knew the answer
to that, and the terror of my utter aloneness and certain
damnation wracked my little life.

Later, when I was licensed to preach (at the wise old age of sixteen), I began to give back what I was given: I used to walk up to people in shopping malls and inform them that they would spend an eternity in unquenchable fire unless they embraced my peculiar religious formula. I cringe today at the thought of it, but the truth was I was driven to do this, too, out of fear. Quoting Ezekiel 33:8 ("If I say to the wicked, 'O wicked ones, you shall surely die,' and you do not speak to warn the wicked to turn from their ways, the wicked shall die in their iniquity, but their blood I will require at your hand") our leaders told us that God would hold us accountable at judgment for every person we came in contact with that we did not proselytize. So, out of fear, I inflicted fear on others, perpetuating a sincere but insidious spiral.

Near the end of my high-school years (when I was called "Rev" and carried a huge red Bible wherever I went) my family and I were disfellowshiped from our church for a variety of petty reasons. I was bitter and very, very hurt. I played the church game a while longer, but I finally renounced the god of my parents and my childhood. Keeping him happy was an impossible and thankless task, and, as a young adult, I was discovering that all of those people whom I had long considered evil and corrupt—namely anyone who wasn't a Baptist—were fine and sensitive people with beliefs and wounds of their own. This was quite a revelation, and I began to avidly explore the faith traditions of others, searching for the "right" one.

Disconcertingly, I discovered that these other traditions also had strict proscriptions of just how one should believe and act, with terrifying descriptions of the eternal consequences of ignoring them that rivaled the vividness of my tradition of origin. Finally, blind drunk at four in the morning in the parking lot of my girlfriend's apartment building, I sank to my knees and screamed up at the heavens, "I don't know who you are—and I cannot accept the god of my parents—but if something is up there, I have to know. Please!"

Within twenty-four hours, I was on a road-trip with my

girlfriend and my best friend B.J. and his wife. I asked B.J. to describe God. B.J. began to describe a magnificent cosmic dance, with all the planets, suns, galaxies, angels, and demons spinning around in a seemingly chaotic but endlessly ornate choreography. Only humankind had forgotten how to dance, and our various faith traditions are our attempts to learn the steps again and rejoin the cosmic shindig. It was the most marvelous and intuitive explanation I had ever heard. Everything in me cried "Aha!" and I wept for two days. I realized that Christianity was my tradition—my place in the Dance—and that I must learn to dance again.

But this time, I would be real. I got my ear pierced as a covenant with God never to fall back into fundamentalist conformity. I would be the first to admit to being a hypocrite, and would do everything in my power to be a person of faith, intellect, and integrity.

Not long after, I went away to California Baptist College, where I had to confront the demons of my childhood faith face to face on a daily basis. I was looked down upon as a sort of bohemian misfit, but in the Humanities Department I found many like-souled friends and compatriots. All seemed to be going well until the nightmares began. I dreamed of hellfire night after night, and would wake up screaming and thrashing (which upset my wife to no end, as one might imagine). I was reaching another point of crisis in my life, when I came upon the Robert Browning poem, "Caliban Upon Setabos."

Caliban, you might recall, is the monster in Shakespeare's *The Tempest*. Setebos is Caliban's name for his god. In the poem, the monster is soliloquizing about how he loves to make other things suffer, and surely Setebos must be the same, reveling in the groveling of the weak before his might, playing with them, squashing them at whim. Caliban fears that he may be ground underfoot as he has done to so many creatures smaller than he. So he grovels, begs the monster god Setebos for more mercy than he himself has ever shown, and envies the might that could very well extinguish him:

> This Caliban strives hard and ails no less,
> And always, above all else, envies Him;
> Wherefore he mainly dances on dark nights,
> Moans in the sun, gets under hoes to laugh,
> And never speaks his mind save housed as now:
> Outside, 'groans, curses. If He caught me here,
> O'erheard this speech, and asked,
>   "What chucklest at?"
> 'Would, to apease Him, cut a finger off,
> Or of my three kid yearlings burn the best,
> Or let the toothsome aples rot on tree,
> Or push my taem beast for the orc to taste:
> While myself lit a fire, and made a song
> And sunt it, "What I hate, be consecrate
> To celebrate Thee and Thy state, no mate
> For Thee; what see for envy in poor me?"

The poem shook me deeply—for the first time someone had dared to speak the awful truth: God was a monster, driven by lusts beyond his control, hell-bent on our misery and destruction.

This had a twofold effect upon me. I realized in a moment of *satori* that repentance born of fear is invalid, and that only love is an acceptable religious motivation. But how can one love a monster? I had no answer to that question at the time. The other effect was that I began to write poetry of my own in which the figure of the Monster God became more and more prominent and well-defined. I was terrified at first of what was pouring out from my pen. The poems came fast, a torrent of rage and violence. The Monster God developed as a fierce but buffoonish caricature wantonly leveling buildings and masticating innocents. At first I had to rename God "Zeus" and Jesus "Apollo" in order to deal with the fear that accompanied these creations.

The final chapter of the Monster God cycle, from my novel-in-odd-verse *The Frog Mentality*, takes the Monster God caricature to the outermost limit:

It was God's Birthday and so we took him to Denny's for dinner. God didn't wait his turn when the time came to order, but thundered out "Thick slabs of meat!" so loud that the waitress picked blood from her ear.

"I'm first!" God slathered at Dad.

"Uh, of course," Dad said nervously, inching closer to Mom and sweating at the neck.

When their meals came God grabbed whatever he wanted from their plates, and not only that, he chewed with his mouth open, making loud "smack, smack" noises.

"Hey!" objected Timmy, but God crushed his head in.

When God got up to go to the bathroom, Sis leaned over and whispered, "What a pig!"

"Well," Mom, flustered, mounted to God's defense. "I'll bet that where God comes from, grabbing, smacking, and murdering the young are the very peak of social etiquette."

"You mean in heaven they chew with their mouths open?" Sis asked.

When dessert was over, God was licking his lips and staring at the food at the next table. Dad turned over the check.

"I'll get that!" God shouted.

"No, it's your birthday...."

"You think I can't pay for this, don't you?" God sneered.

"No, not at all, it's just that...."

"Well, I'll teach you a thing or two!" God reared and splattered Dad's head across the paned glass.

"Oh, how beastly!" Sis piped indignantly.

"Beastly? What? Fuck off!" God said and stuck his thumb through her head.

"I'm a nice guy," he breathed to the horrified clientele, "and don't forget it. And don't forget to tell your kids. 'Cause if you do...." and he rambled off a deluxe assortment of threats.

"Can't take him anywhere...." Mom sobbed.

"I heard that!" God sneered.

Eventually I began to make an internal distinction between the God of my true and heartfelt devotion and the Monster God of my childhood. The true Mother of the Universe was not the Tasmanian Devil of my nightmares, but the full internalization of this distinction was still a long time in coming.

After many years of study, and the completion of my doctoral work in philosophy and religion, I have again turned to the subject that has stalked me all of my life. In researching the history of the Monster God, I found the evolution of an idea, not the biography of a person. In this book I stare the Monster God in the face, and explore the many facets of his personality, displaying him naked in all of his glory and his shame.

With this book I have turned a significant corner in my journey. I have also found that this journey is not mine alone. I was not the only child to cower before the specter of a malignant deity. The image of the Monster God has been haunting us for as long as we have cringed at the crack of thunder. The idea that the being that controls all things might not only contain the capacity for evil, but might in fact *be* evil creates a cognitive dissonance that is difficult for us to resolve, and has kept the human imagination busy creating a variety of fabulous theologies and theories to account for this awful contradiction. Not only does it shake us intellectually, but psychologically it undermines our hope and moves us to apathy and despair.

Of course, I am no stranger to these feelings. I know them intimately, and this book is the result of such dangerous and tender knowledge. This is a "small book," and I am not attempting an exhaustive treatise on the subject. It is my goal only to explore ideas about the Monster God in a few choice traditions. But it will be clear, when we are finished, that this deity is part and parcel of the human experience, from the very earliest glimmerings of spiritual intuition.

I will explore this darker aspect of the divine in many of the world's native traditions, as well as in each of the three dominant religions in the West: Judaism, Christianity and Islam, with a brief foray into Zoroastrianism. I have also chosen to focus on the mythologies of the Hindus, for although the monster gods are found in nearly every culture of the world, few have celebrated them to the extent that India has.

Within each of these contexts, I shall examine the nature of evil, what precisely it is that evokes the ire of the gods; the gods of wrath, whose violence and anger have left a trail of destruction; the gods of betrayal, who tempt and trick humankind into being the objects of their wrath; the gods of rape, whose violation is supreme; the gods of genocide, whose destruction is absolute; the gods of judgment, whose unforgiving nature compels them to punish dissidents in unspeakable and eternal ways; and finally, the shadow of God, the dualistic projection which we have named Satan, the cosmic scapegoat upon whose head the sins of God are carried into the wilderness, or the "outer darkness." Finally we shall examine the implications of the Monster God for people of faith, and attempt a reconciliation of God with us.

This study has been a profoundly personal one, but it is also the journey of all peoples of faith for whom the immensity of God has proven more daunting than comforting. It is the result of the existential terror of a random universe, of the void, and of the spiritual coercion of others. It is the evil chapter of the bible of humankind, lending us license through the ages to be as merciless, unrepentant, and destructive as the Monster Gods we have served.

My experiences with the Monster God have not been extraordinary. I have not suffered major loss in my life. I have known no holocausts. The stories told in the Fundamentalists Anonymous group I ran several years ago are very like my own. My experiences are most ordinary, which leads me to believe that there are many who have lived as "sinners in the hands of an angry God." In fact, I have no doubt that history is also full of them, especially in light of the myths and legends that follow.

Today, at this stage in my journey, I find that I am a man who struggles with belief, but also one who aches with great hope. Faith comes to me only as a result of great mental effort. I still find comfort and meaning in my tradition, but I do not approach it uncritically or unreservedly. I know where my home is, but just as my native country is not without its political and social evils, my native faith is likewise riddled with spiritual ones. I have learned to talk back to God, to hold the Ancient of Days accountable for what role "he" might have played in the world's misery, but I am also concerned that the blame rest in its proper place. These are by no means resolved issues, and this book offers no resolution. But I believe that within its pages you will find the horror you always knew was there, but whose name you were forbidden to speak. And I wish to offer what hope I have found for living in the shadow of an angry God.

JRM
January, 2006
Pt. Richmond, CA

Wherefore should God be wroth at thy voice,
and destroy the work of thy hands?

Ecclesiastes 5:6
Darby Bible

Chapter One

The Ire of the Gods

As a child in Sunday School, I was puzzled by a fact that caused me a great deal of distress: God gets angry. Usually the Sunday School teacher had a good explanation for this: the inhabitants of Sodom and Gomorrah were wicked; so were the people of the whole earth prior to the flood; the people of Israel were fickle, worshipping the gods of their neighbors. The scriptures also spoke of God's anger towards Israel's enemies (which, at least in my Sunday School classes, was clearly understandable). But growing up in a home where any display of rage was surely punishable, God came across to this child as rather childish, and I was sure that my parents would not tolerate such behavior if God were living in *our* house.

When I grew up and began to study the mythologies of other traditions, Yahweh's behavior did not seem so unusual. The gods are funny people. One minute they can put you on the top of the world, make you invincible, give you great glory and wealth, and in the next, dash you to your ruin. Poets have written innumerable pages through the eons describing their fickleness, and staying on their good side has been one of humankind's primary concerns.

But exactly what it is that upsets the gods has changed as the gods have changed (though the desire to stay on their good side is constant enough). Historians of religion have divided human religious evolution into three discreet stages. In each, the motivations of the gods are drastically different, and so also are the methods human beings have used in coping with these celestial hotheads. Let's take a look at each of these stages in turn.

Primordial Religion[1]

The first stage in humankind's spiritual evolution is one in which our ancestors lived in small groups with a single, cohesive view of reality. This reality was filled with magic and spirits, and presented a world that might seem familiar to many of us when we recall our childhoods.

One of my earliest memories is of a very long night watching the closet. I was about three and a half, as close as I can figure, and when the lights were turned off, I perceived a glowing presence in amongst my shirts and jackets. Repeated cries to Mother brought a flick of the light (the ghost, of course, whipping out of sight) and a dismissive search of the room for the "bogeys." Then the light would go off, and the presence would re-emerge. In the course of the night, I clearly discerned the features of the ghost. What did it want with me? What had I done to deserve being haunted? I stayed awake and stared him, her, or it down for many hours until fatigue overcame adrenaline.

What strikes me about this memory is that, forty years later, it is still extremely vivid. I remember the scene exactly, but most of all I remember my feelings: panic, dread, and eventually resignation.

Perhaps it is so clear to me even today because the experience is a primal one. Fear of the "things that go bump in the night" is a universal aspect of being human. We fear what we do not know. Darkness impedes our ability to know, it disempowers us and leaves us defenseless against the unknown.

The famed Danish explorer Rasmussen was stumped during one of his many interviews with Native American "Eskimos" when one of them suddenly turned the tables on him and asked,

Why must there be snow and storms and bad weather for hunting, for us who must hunt for our daily food, who seek meat for ourselves and those we love? Why must hunters, after they have slaved all day, return without a catch? Why must the children of my neighbor sit shivering huddled under a skin-rug, hungry? Why must my old sister suffer pain at the ending of her days? She has done no wrong that we can see but lived her many years and given birth to good strong children.

I am sure that Rasmussen believed this to be an angry rant, and was probably not prepared for the answer that followed:

We fear! We fear the elements with which we have to fight in their fury to wrest our food from land and sea. We fear cold and famine in our snow huts. We fear the sickness that is daily to be seen among us. Not death, but the suffering. We fear the souls of the dead, of human and animal alike. We fear the spirits of earth and air. And therefore our fathers, taught by their fathers before them, guarded themselves about with all these old rules and customs, which are built upon the experience and knowledge of generations. We don't know how or why, but we obey them that we may be suffered to live in peace. And for all our [shamans] and their knowledge of hidden things, we yet know so little that we fear everything else.[2]

For this Native American, both fear and mystery appear to be at the core of life. The looming immensity of the unknown, the uncertainty of survival, and the tragedies of the past all conspired in this man, making him feel powerless in the face of cruel and impersonal circumstance.

I grieve that for the great majority of our history we have not remembered the names of those who suffered and died. We do not remember the tales of heroism and sacrifice, the myriad tragedies of our grandmothers and grandfathers. They might have words very similar to the Native American quoted above. They might have told us: Mystery is our sworn enemy.

Our problem is that Mystery is bigger than we are. What humankind cannot control it must be content to persuade. Our ancestors were powerless over starvation, disease, and death, and it only seems natural that they would seek means to control in an occult fashion what they could not manipulate physically. The beginning of religion is the first toddling step towards putting a face on the gaping maw of time, and giving humanity some influence as to its own fate; some hope for survival, or at best, meager comfort.[3]

It took a long time, however, before any recognizable concept of divinity emerged. Our ancestors first intuited that there was a force, a power, latent in nature which is the origin of "luck" or supernatural good fortune—or for that matter, bad fortune. The Melanesian islanders called this power "*mana*," and scholars of religion have followed suit.

Mana was not perceived as being in any way "super-natural." *Mana* was an element of the natural world, of which our ancestors also recognized themselves a part. *Mana* was the controllable and perceptible "force" that was part of a world brimming with—and beleaguered by—Mystery. Children grew up in a world where rocks, trees, animals, people, and *mana* were all equal and unquestioned facts of daily life.

But daily life was hard. For every success, a tragedy was not far behind. Our forebears did not have the precedent of Greek philosophy to separate the world into categories of the real and the ideal. There was only what they saw with their eyes, and perceived with their own acute intuition. The world was a mixture of pleasure and pain, an undifferentiated tangle of positive and negative impressions. People were good, and people were bad, much as the weather. *Mana*, not surprisingly, shared this ambivalence.

Mana could be good, causing the grain to grow and relations to be congenial. But *mana* could also be bad, causing disease and strife. Our ancestors naturally sought to inspire and make use of good *mana* through the use of incantations or charms, while devising rituals of purification to be rid of negative *mana*, and by doing this they constructed our first metaphysical "tools."

Like the ghost in my closet, whom I was sure was haunting me for a specific reason, our forebears eventually began to discern personality in *mana*, and began to speak of the "powers" as individual entities like themselves, with feelings and motivations of their own. These became the "spirits," the *numina* that indwelt all things around them. The dryads and naiads of classical mythology are remnants from this stage. The spirits had minds of their own, and could easily be more destructive than helpful. Our ancestors devised ways to persuade them to behave, or to entreat them to help in difficult situations by offering gifts.

For them, the spirits were an aspect of everyday life; part of the family that must be lived with, made peace with, and at times coerced into doing one's bidding. These spirits were as much part of the forest as humankind, and although possessed of magical powers, and worthy of fear, they were perceived to be locals, part of the scenery, and not above, or ruling over, humanity. Sometimes, in fact, they were seen as the ancestors themselves, the spirits of the departed. By means of magic, humankind attempted to temper nature and the spirits, enlisting their cooperation, and sometimes coercing them in order to keep their people safe and plentiful. Chinese culture even today retains this fear of the harm ancestors might wreck upon a family's status.

At this stage in our collective history, ethics as a philosophical category did not exist. Evil was thought of as that which threatened the well-being of the community: the wild forces of nature that bring disaster and drought, and those persons and spirits that may harm or kill members of the tribe and so endanger its survival. The ethics of our ancestors could probably be summed up simply: That which helps the people to survive is good; that which endangers them is evil.

Polytheistic Religion

This scene shifted dramatically when our ancestors became farmers. No longer content with the insecurity of hunting and gathering, but longing to gain greater control of their future, our forebears were willing to sacrifice the freedom and autonomy of nomadic life for greater economic security. People became connected to the land in a way that was unknown before. Land became the instrument of survival, and the chief commodity to be seized and controlled. As various tribes began to conquer each other, and sought to regulate communities distant from their own, the leap was made from the local to the universal. Suddenly it was not enough to rule one's own people: an early impulse toward manifest destiny declared that the more people one ruled over, the better chance one's tribe had of survival. So chiefs became kings, and the people became subjects.

Not content to leave their spirits in the dust, theological speculation traveled along similar lines. The spirits became gods, ruling like kings over vast spaces in heaven and on earth. Instead of being the "spirits of the grove," and local neighbors, the gods became distant monarchs residing on the far and noble mountaintop or even in the heavens. This shift inaugurates polytheism in the history of humankind's religious development.

Often the line between Primordial and Polytheistic religion is blurry at best. There are steps toward transcendence, and yet the fascination and interaction with nature powers is maintained, sometimes within the same system of belief. For instance, among several African tribes along the Nile, there is the idea of *jok*, which can be a name for the spirits, the gods, beings from another world, the Creator God, or even (most recently) the Holy Ghost (as used by Christian missionaries). According to these tribes, someone who is very lucky is *jok*, while someone who has suffered misfortunes has "angry *jok*." Europeans appeared to be magical because of their technology, and so, of course, they were *jok*. A wounded beast is *jok*, as well.[4]

"*Jok* is the unified spirit of God and the gods, personal and impersonal, local and omnipresent," says one historian of mythology.[5] Such ambivalence towards categorization is not uncommon amongst tribes "in transition" between the Primordial and Polytheistic stages.

While such holdovers inevitably remain, much of humanity's relation to the *numen* nevertheless changed drastically. The spirits were now writ large, and had to be propitiated in the same way as human kings. The gods could not be coerced or controlled by magic. For our ancestors, success or failure in controlling the spirits rested in one's competence as a magician or a medicine person. It was the shaman who decided what must be done, and drew upon his or her traditions of ritual magic to manipulate the spirits, and to effect their behavior. In Polytheistic religion, however, humankind no longer felt they could directly coerce the spirits, and so a person's success lay with how pious he or she could be. The means of manipulating the gods thus shifted from control to persuasion. But as the deities came to be conceived of as kings, people had to be as respectful and discreet in their methods as they would be towards any earthly ruler. Rituals became longer, and more elaborate. Formal places of worship were built and a class of professional clergy emerged.

Even with all of the ritual machinery in place, however, we cannot expect the gods to behave themselves. Like any earthly ruler, the gods could be petty and childish. Floods, earthquakes, plagues, and other disasters were all taken to be signs of the gods' wrath, before which human beings could only cower. As when dealing with any abusive parent, any protest may well bring further ruin.

Evil in polytheistic traditions was still thought of, by and large, in terms of social evil, of what endangers the community. But it was not mischievous spirits with which our ancestors had then to contend, but the evil of the gods.

Service of the gods was still a matter of survival for polytheistic people, to keep the evil of starvation or sickness away, but many of the gods had their own ideas about what evil was— namely whatever might threaten their power, or, perhaps with some justification, the order of the cosmos. Most importantly, humankind was to keep in its place. Heaven was for the gods and the gods alone.

We hear echoes of this in early Hebrew mythology, where the serpent deceives Adam and Eve into thinking that they can become "as gods"; and also in the divine judgment meted out at the Tower of Babel. God is the ruler, the people are serfs, and never the twain shall meet. Or as Apollo says in the *Iliad*, "Never shall they be like each other, the tribe of immortal gods and the tribe of men that walk upon the earth."

Folklorist Jacob Grimm pointed out that such a situation often provokes a "rebellious spirit in men, which breaks out in promethean defiance and threats, or even takes a violent turn."[6] Such is the stuff of good, roiling mythology, but it also belies humanity's frustration with the apparent callousness of the gods. Humanity had over time built up for itself complex edifices of ritual and story to enable them to cope with the uncertainties and tragedies of daily life, yet tragedy seemed never to be too remote, and the gods seemed deaf to entreaty, even monstrous at times in their capriciousness and wrath.

Monotheistic Religion

The universalizing trend begun in Polytheism continued to snowball in humanity's imagination, leading to a whole new stage in religious development. This third stage was ushered in with the notion that there is a single, creative personality behind the cosmos, and, later, that this being must be "absolute" and "perfect." This transition from polytheism to monotheism, from plurality to monism, was, of course, not an overnight occurrence. Hinduism provides an excellent example of a single tradition that began as polytheistic (the Vedic period) and struggled and stretched its way into the qualified monotheism of later Hinduism (sometimes called Upanishadic Hinduism), accumulating along the way an enormous and conflicting body of mythology in which the complexity and terror of the gods know few equals in the mythologies of other peoples. The Hindu gods' struggle against evil is a unique one, and serves to illustrate humanity's religious evolution in an exemplary manner.

For the Hindu, evil is a relative term. At least in primitive Hinduism, there were few absolutes. None of the gods were purely moral, nor were many purely evil. And in later Hinduism, since the universe is One, and since all happenings were in the service of the greater good, the illusion of evil was the necessary catalyst to keep the universe moving in God's intended direction.

All things, including evil, had a divine — if not entirely auspicious — origin. There are many myths recounting the origin of evil as being an expelation from the body of the Creator, usually from the penis or rectum. In one relatively late Hindu scripture we learn that "evil spirits arise from Krishna's private part, his penis or anus, and injury, misfortune, death, and hell derive from the rectum of the creator."[6] Elsewhere we find that human beings are the feces of Brahma, and the demons, his passed gas.[8]

In earlier myths, it is the primeval god Prajapati from whose body evil arises:

In the beginning, Prajapati was alone and wanted to procreate; seeking in vain a second, a female, he saw the Brahmin and asked him to procreate with him, but the Brahmin refused, saying, "No, for you are the grasp of evil; evil is upon your head." At Prajapati's request, the Brahmin bound him at the nape of the neck, the waist, and the ankles, and with three strokes got rid of the evil for him. The evil was then divided into threefold prosperity, and placed in the cow, in sleep, and in shadow. Then Prajapati heated himself in order to create.[9]

A case of taking lemons and making divine lemonade if there ever was one, this myth suggests that there is little moral attachment to evil. Like *mana* of Primordial religions, evil is essentially a force, a power, whose ethical boundaries are fluid, and which can be applied for good or ill. The Hindu universe, it is important to note, is a closed box: there is a fixed amount of everything, especially power. As Wendy Doniger O'Flaherty describes it,

> ...more here necessarily implies less there. God must be powerful in order for the universe (including [hu]mankind) to remain alive and to function properly; and he must rid himself of his sin in order to remain in power. The evil god must be kept powerful, no matter how evil he becomes; for though sin does not negate divinity, the loss of power does.[10]

Hinduism is similar in this perspective to native traditions. It is not their own malevolence which endangers the gods, but weakness. Evil is whatever disempowers divinity, while good is whatever protects and promotes it. The demons of the Vedic period (early Hinduism) are demonic not because they are necessarily cruel, but because they are the gods' rivals for power. In later Hinduism, when the practices of extreme asceticism and sacrifice guaranteed human beings a certain degree of control over the universe, the focus of the gods' insecurity shifted from the demonic to the human. People became the objects of the gods' suspicion, moving them to trick people, to undermine their holiness (and therefore power) by means of moral sabotage, visiting upon humankind such horrors as sleep, sloth, anger, hunger, and a lust for gambling.[11]

In the Mahabharata, Hinduism's greatest epic poem, we learn

that men were full of *dharma* — which can mean truth, or cosmic
law. This frightened the gods because such an accumulation of
dharma would allow humankind to become gods themselves. The
gods sought the counsel of the creator god, Brahma. Taking pity
on their situation, Brahma enacted a magical ritual and produced
a delusion which would eradicate the virtue of men — women!
Brahma filled this new variety of human with wanton desires, so
that the men began to lust after them, bringing desire and anger
in its wake.[12]

The gods are in no hurry to eradicate evil, then, for when
human beings fall into sin they are disempowered, and are
therefore less of a threat. Paradoxically, it is the righteous and holy
persons, their greatest devotees, who pose the chief threat to the
gods. If human beings sin, they are in the clutches of the demons,
and are of no concern to the gods. But if a righteous man has built
up spiritual power through prayers and asceticism, and is familiar
with the laws of the universe, then he becomes a danger.

On the other hand, the gods cannot completely alienate
human beings, because they need people to feed them through
their daily sacrifices. This tension, this clutching and pushing
away, is a common theme in Hindu mythology, making clear that
the purpose of evil in early Hinduism is two-fold: to keep
humanity in check, and to create intolerable situations that will
force humanity to keep honoring the gods and sacrificing to
them.

Since, in the Hindu universe, all creatures are capable of
cosmic power, we may well ask to what extent we puny humans
might possibly threaten the gods. What separates humanity from
divinity? One middle period Hindu scripture says, "At first, the
gods were like men. They wished to dispel need, evil, and death,
and to reach the place of the gods. And they did."[13] The possibility of humanity becoming like them was, of course, an intolerable danger for the gods, and they sought to pollute humanity
while ridding themselves of their own sin. In contrast to

Christianity, and many later Hindu myths where God takes the sins of the world upon himself in order to liberate humanity, the gods of the Vedic period cast their own sin onto humanity in order to enslave it. There are numerous myths recounting how the gods removed various impurities from themselves—including death—and invested them in humankind, leaving us mortal, and essentially at their mercy. Therefore, in order for the gods to be good, we must become evil. It becomes the almost insane mission of humanity, in this system, to be the salvation of the gods.

As for the demons, they were not always inferior to the gods. At one time they were, in fact, their superiors, their elders from whom the gods wrested heaven. The Kathaka Samhita says, "The gods and demons performed the sacrifice; whatever the gods did, the demons did. The demons were greater, and better; the gods were younger and more evil, like younger brothers. Then the gods saw the first part of the Soma libation and grabbed it, and with it they became first."[14]

According to the Mahabharata, the gods and the demons used to live in peace. Then, they joined forces to churn the ocean and create the elixir of immortality. By means of trickery the gods claimed this elixir as their own and the demons were denied. As a result the demons became mortal, and were only a continuing threat due to their prolific breeding. Since only one side could have the elixir, the incident set in place forever the enmity between the elder and younger deities.

In the Vedic period, it was the demons who posed the chief threat to the gods, and so the gods and humanity often strove together against them. This situation did not last, however, but changed when Vedic sacrifices gave way to the practice of asceticism and meditation in the Upanishadic period. During this time we begin to see myths emerge from the perspective of human beings—specifically the priestly caste (Brahmins) who saw their ministry as more important to the survival of the universe than the gods!

With the advent of power through *tapas* (the raising of spiritual power through ascetic practice) the demons in the Brahmanic period were able to gain power in the same way as humans, through spiritual practice, regardless of their ends or intent. Just as human beings were a threat to the gods due to their ascetic virtue, virtuous and ascetic demons were more dangerous than evil ones. The variety of power-struggles in this later period of Hindu development often makes for some very confused cycles of myths, and adds to the rich kaleidoscopic contributions of Hindu mythology to the history of religion.

When our attention shifts to the Abrahamic religions (Judaism, Christianity, and Islam), however, the problem of evil becomes much simpler in terms of "who-is-mad-at-who," although much more complex in terms of logical rationalization.

For the God of Israel, evil is primarily a matter of disobedience. In the book of Deuteronomy, the Israelites are told:

See, I am setting before you today a blessing and a curse: the blessing, if you obey the commandments of the LORD your God that I am commanding you today; and the curse, if you do not obey the commandments of the LORD your God, but turn from the way that I am commanding you today, to follow other gods that you have not known.[15]

This theme is shared by Christianity, as evidenced by St. Paul's warning, "Let no one deceive you with empty words, for because of these things the wrath of God comes on those who are disobedient."[16]

This gives human beings a certain amount of control over God: as long as we are obedient, God will be happy with us and no misfortune will befall us. Yet, as the book of Job attests, life rarely works out so neatly. Bad things still happen to good people. Human beings suffer God's wrath for no apparent reason, and the will of this "perfect" deity often seems elusive and labyrinthine.

Evil in the Abrahamic traditions is also logically problematic. Explaining the existence of evil in a world where the gods themselves are evil is easy; explaining evil in a world where the divinity is supposed to be perfect has sent theologians into fits for centuries. The mental gymnastics employed to resolve the dilemma are reminiscent of the medieval "How many angels can dance on the head of a pin?" questions, and are nearly as useful. The position with the most integrity has been held by those theologians bold enough to simply say "We don't know how God does it. It's a mystery."

Few believers are truly happy with this solution, however. Most people need to have "the answers" to feel secure, to contend with the shrouded uncertainty that is the one rule of our lives. For the people of the late twentieth century, knowledge is power. If something is known, it can be controlled and conquered. Powerless-ness is our greatest terror. That which is unknown is always a threat, whether in the form of an unidentifiable virus or the secret plans of the enemy general. If this is so (and I think it is) then the arch-nemesis of humankind is still Mystery.

This of course, leaves us where we began. Powerless in the face of the unknown. After millennia of spinning tales to satisfy our questions about ultimate reality, in the end, we are left wordless, standing gape-jawed in the face of the void, our mythologies and theologies so much useless detritus at our feet. Mystery is our beginning and our ending. It is the great evil that must be overcome, even at the cost of reason.

What makes God angry? What acts elicit storms and other natural disasters? Whose arm lends might to the tyrant? What misdeed provokes the plague? How can sorrow be averted? What can we do to sway the divine will to suffer us to live?

We will never know the answers to these questions. But we can explore the human need that gives them birth. And we can meditate upon the wrath of the gods we imagine must be the cause of such tragedies. In the following chapters we will stare fearlessly into the faces of angry gods, gods of wrath, betrayal, genocide, and rape. In them we may not find the authentic face of the divine at all, but if we are honest, and we endure, we may indeed find the origin of evil.

Do not strike us in our sons or in the length of our life.
Be not cruel! Do not injure us in our cattle or our horses.
Do not slay our brave men in your anger, O lord of tears!

Svetasvatara Upanishad 4.22

Chapter Two

The Gods of Wrath

My parents believe in the power of the belt. They take the biblical injunction, "spare the rod and spoil the child" (Proverbs 13:24) literally, and whenever I would introduce a new girlfriend, my mother would always take me aside and ask, "Does she believe in spanking?" as if that question was the litmus test of good parenting. Because I experienced my father's wrath at the end of a belt often, I never had any trouble projecting that willingness to physically punish onto God.

That God is full of wrath hardly seems a debatable point in our culture. Evangelical talk shows speculate regularly as to the divine origins of various disasters: the AIDS epidemic is God's just wrath upon homosexuals, Hurricane Katrina was divine retaliation against the "sin city" of the South, New Orleans. The White House declared the war in Iraq to be God's righteous punishment for the 9/11 attacks, and jingoistic pundits followed suit. Naysayers were ignored, and the general public entirely missed the irony inherent in declaring Holy War on those who declare Holy War against us. The Islamic rhetoric against the hedonism and atheism of the West is just as heated. Many of those who do not believe the terrorists are in the right still quietly believe that the West deserves what is coming to it. Every new natural disaster brings with it the obligatory question, "why?" and for countless millions of true believers around the world, the answer must always be because, for some reason, God wills it.

How did we get to this point? We know from our last chapter that the gods get mad, but what would move them to vent their wrath against human beings, creatures so small and vulnerable as to be almost beneath their notice? The injustice of the powerful man taking off his belt and venting his frustration upon a defenseless child is here writ large. What possible justice is served, and what relief gained for divinity by such wonton destruction of the weak by the unimaginably strong?

The Hungry Spirits
of Primordial Religion

The answer began, once again, in the Primordial stage of religious development. The earliest wrathful gods were undoubtedly the spirits of the ancestors who did not find rest, or were not properly and respectfully remembered. Amongst the Mongo-Nkudo of Zaire, these spirits are referred to as *biloko* (singular *eloko*), dwarf-spirits who have lived before but still have a score to settle with the living. As Jan Knappert described them, "They live in hollow trees and are dressed only in leaves. They have no hair; only grass grows on their bodies; they have piercing eyes, snouts with mouths that can be opened wide enough to admit a human body, alive or dead, and long, sharp claws."[1] The *biloko* also possess little bells which bewitch passersby, who, unless armed with a powerful amulet, cannot withstand their allure.

In one story, a hunter was being badgered by his wife to take her deep into the forest, where he had built a "get-away" hut for them. One day he had to go out into the forest to inspect the traps he was keeping, and he warned her, "If you hear a bell ringing, freeze! Those *bilokos* love to eat wives for dinner. You'll die if you move!" With this admonition, he trudged off on his rounds. Not long after, his wife heard the inviting tinkle of a little bell. It was getting louder and louder, until the bell seemed just outside the door of the hut. A kindly voice asked permission to enter, and it sounded to her like a child. So she opened the door and looked down upon a tiny *eloko*, who grinned up at her innocently. Wanting to be hospitable, the woman offered the "child" some porridge and fish, but the *eloko* refused it, saying, "No, we only eat people. I am very hungry, and I believe you will now give me your arm to eat." The woman was by now completely under the *eloko*'s hypnotic command, and she offered the little demon her own flesh. Later that evening, when the hunter returned, he found not his wife, but only a small pile of bones.[2]

Evil spirits with distinct personalities abound in Africa, with a different spirit responsible for almost every known disease—the impulse to blame illnesses on the deities goes back a lot further than the AIDS crisis. Sometimes the actions of the spirits are the result of anger, but usually, it is just their natures to be nasty. Such spirits are referred to by some as *buso*, beings that send fatal diseases upon people, and then feed on their corpses once they are dead.[3]

A development of the *buso* spirits is Tagamaling, from the mythology of the Bagobo people, and it is here that we really see the transformation of the malevolent nature spirits into the exalted status of divinity. Tagamaling began his tenure as one of the malignant *buso* spirits, and was later "reclassified" as a more benevolent sort, since he only eats people every other month. On the months when he is dining on humans, he is considered *buso*, but in the off months, he is revered as a god. It is easy to tell when danger is afoot—Tagamaling only eats humans during the dark of the moon.[4]

In northern Africa, *buso* are more likely to be known as *jinn*, which are well known to most of us in the West through their Islamicized form in the Arabian Nights stories. *Jinn* are spirits who can assume any form they please, and can travel instantaneously to any place on earth. Morally, *jinn* are ambivalent. Some are merely mischievous, while others are downright evil. Muslims would later describe the cause of their moral fall as their predilection for copulating with creatures of other species, resulting in their frequent appearance as horribly misshapen mixtures with hooves, fur, snouts, and horns.[5]

The *buso* and *jinn* represent a relatively late period of Primordial religious development, and are not yet the transcendent gods of power and might so familiar to us. The Edo people of Nigeria, however, developed a dualism that separated the good gods from one particular nasty character, Ogiuwu.

The Edo believed Ogiuwu to be the cause of death, and to appease him human sacrifices were made at his temple in Benin City. According to legend, Ogiuwu is the lawful owner of the blood of all beings, and it is said that his palace in the Other World is painted red with it. He never emerges from his dread estate, but instead sends his own grim-reaper-for-hire out to do his dirty work—a horrifying creature known as Ofoe.

Ofoe appears as a human head on two legs, fast enough to pursue any fleeing human, and long arms that suffer no escape. Though Ogiuwo may be appeased, apparently once Ofoe has been sent out, the deal is done. As the locals warn, "Ofoe has no mercy and yields to no sacrifices."[6]

The Greek equivalent of such mischievous spirits survived into the Polytheistic period in the form of the myths of the furies, or the Erinyes, the spirits of anger and revenge.[7] Michael Macrone describes their function:

The notion of such Furies...was vague at first, but already in Homer's work they have two specific jobs: punishing the shades of evil men in Tartarus and effecting curses on Earth. Later writers decided there were exactly three of them...and that they were grim, if beautiful, deities clad in black, whose eyes dripped blood, whose hair was tangled with serpents, and whose weapon of choice was the scourge. While they may have literally lashed the "bodies" of evil shades, they tormented the living psychologically—that is, they personified guilt, or at least what approximated guilt in early Greek society.[8]

While these wrathful nature spirits are certainly fierce, there is little evidence that their actions are in the service of some higher justice. Most of these dangerous lesser spirits wreck their havoc not to punish humans but to simply feed themselves. From the *buso* that ate the hunter's wife to Ogiuwu who feeds on the blood of human sacrifices, these spirits are only mirroring the law of tooth and nail so evident in every arena of primitive life. These spirits are no different from the tigers, panthers, or indeed, the wily deadliness of human hunters who must kill to eat. The difference is that, in the case of the *buso* and other dangerous spirits, humans are the food. The furies are the exception to this rule, and in them we see moral judgment enter the picture for the first time. It is an idea that would catch on in a very big way.

The Wrathful Gods in Polytheistic Religions

As we move into the Polytheistic era of religious development, the spirits become the gods, and in this transition they become more removed, more powerful, and more inexplicable in their dealings with humans and with each other. Few of the gods are purely evil, but they are self-absorbed and primarily concerned with their own best interests. Sometimes they even appear to be ordinary folks having a really bad day, like the Hittite god, Telepinu. As Donna Rosenberg tells the story:

One day Telepinu, the god who made living things fertile, became furious and shouted, "I am so angry! No one should come near me!" He was so upset that he tried to put his right shoe upon his left foot and his left shoe upon his right foot. This made him even angrier.

Finally he fixed his shoes and stalked off. He took with him the ripening grain, the fertile winds, and the abundant growth in fields, meadows, and grassy plains. He went into the country and wandered into a secluded meadow that was sheltered among a grove of trees. There exhaustion overcame him, and he fell asleep.

Telepinu's rage upset the entire world of nature. Mist swirled over the countryside, fogging the windows of houses. Smoke invaded people's homes. In their fireplaces, the logs smoldered and would not burn. The sheep in the pens and the cattle in the barns ignored each other. The lambs and the calves were even neglected by their mothers. Cattle, sheep, and people no longer conceived. Even those already pregnant with new life could not give birth.

Corn, wheat, and barley no longer grew in the fields. All vegetation withered and died. Without moisture, the mountains and hills dried up. The trees also dried up and could bring forth no fresh growth. The pastures became parched, and the springs evaporated. Famine arose in the land; both human beings and gods feared that they would all die of starvation.[9]

Tilpinu's anger was finally eased at the urging of the goddess of healing and the prayer of humankind. We aren't told why he was in such a rage, just that his wrath was so great that even the gods quailed at the sound of him. Yet Tilpinu wasn't always enraged, but was subject to the same mood swings and spells of irrationality as the human beings who created him in their own image. This story is reminiscent of the effects of Demeter's fury when her daughter Persephone was kidnapped by Hades and demonstrates the gods' "control" over weather and the workings of the cosmos.

Many mythologists see the association of the gods with weather as a major turning point in a society's religious development. In many mythologies the god associated with thunder — that most surprising and terrifying of meteorological events — is seen as chief, or at least a very powerful figure, amongst the gods. This is certainly true of Zeus, Jupiter, and the Norse gods Thor and Wotan (depending on the source). Grimm says that "thunder is especially ascribed to an angry and avenging god... In a thunderstorm the people say to their children: 'the gracious god is angry,' [and in other places] 'God is out there scolding.'"[10] This is the birth of the angry sky god, with whom we still must make our peace in even the most modern of religious expressions. It is the beginning of the perception of the gods as distant, rather than immediate forces, and many societies would be just as happy if they would keep their distance.

Many native African religions, for example, see almost all divine intervention in negative terms, and believe that humans are in the deity's good graces when the deity simply leaves them alone. Any divine visitation whatsoever is likely to be seen as a very bad sign, and even today people believe that when even a benevolent god comes too near, illness, madness and death are not far behind. Therefore the people beg the gods to be merciful and to keep their distance. For some African religions, the best god is an absent god, and the fervent prayers of most of the faithful are for the gods to simply go away.[11]

With the advent of such "high gods," stories began to arise that focused on the creation of the earth and of humankind as the product of a divine agent from outside of the world. This would have been an absurd notion for Primordial believers, for whom the earth and the universe are synonymous. But in the Polytheistic era, people began to discern that a sky god is probably powerful enough to stoop down and fashion, as any artisan might, "his" creation. Of course, this also means that such a deity also possesses the power to destroy in equal proportion, and mythology is rife with stories of angry gods being violent time and again when their great plans have gone awry.

In a Mayan myth (which echoes many on this hemisphere), whenever one of the gods tried to exalt himself above his brothers, the world became somehow tainted, and it and all that lies within it had to be destroyed, whether by water, fire, or wind.[12]

Spider Woman, of the Navajo mythos, was determined not to let this fate befall the fourth, and current world. Spider Woman and her siblings learned from the Sun, their father, how to vanquish the monsters that plagued the Fourth World. After that, however, she settled down to a quiet life of frightening children. According to Page Bryant, "Spider Woman came to live on Earth atop the tallest of the two needles of Spider Rock. Talking God lives on the smaller needle and informs her of the Earth children who misbehave, resulting in her spinning a web and going down and snatching the bad children and, after carrying them back to her home, eating them up."[13]

For most Polytheistic peoples, survival was a matter of being careful not to offend the gods, and appeasing them when they appeared upset. The Mesopotamian pantheon could be particularly nasty. The god Marduk had a tablet that decreed what was to be for every person, but its news was almost always bad. Since different gods governed different activities, it was almost a full-time job to make sure that the proper deity was appeased for everything a person wanted to do. In an interesting reversal from the good feelings we have come to associate with the Jewish Sabbath, the Mesopotamian Sabbath (a day of the week known, interestingly, as Sin) was the one day a week a person did not want to do anything, because all was doomed to failure if attempted on that day.[14]

The gods were rarely just in their dealings with humans, nor were they terribly concerned for the trials and pains of humankind. As Hugh Lloyd-Jones makes clear in *The Justice of Zeus,*

The gods lie for ever, and meet with little but good fortune; men either meet with nothing but ill fortune or at best are given a mixed lot; after death, their existence in Hades will hardly be an existence. Zeus may be father of gods and men in the sense that he is their ruler; but men in general are not the children of Zeus.... In the *Iliad*...the gods look on men with disdain mingled with slight pity... "Nothing," says Zeus himself, "is more wretched than a man, of all things that breathe and move upon the earth."[15]

And yet, for all their disdain of humankind, the gods still want to be praised and worshipped, and were likely to exact a terrific revenge upon those who deprived them of their due adoration and service. As Lloyd-Jones writes, "If Niobe speaks slightly of Leto, if Oeneus omits, whether thorough forgetfulness or ignorance, a sacrifice due to Artemis, if Agamemnon offends Apollo by refusing to release the daughter of his priest, the god will show no mercy."[16] Lloyd-Jones also notes that, terrible as that might seem to us (and for that matter, to Plato) most of the poets felt the gods, by virtue of their status and power (certainly not their ethics), were perfectly within their rights.

If the people were terrified of turning the gods against them, still they delighted in tales of conflict between the gods themselves. The most nefarious and celebrated of the malevolent Egyptian gods is Set, who harbored no great love for his divine relatives. Set was also the god who punishes sinners;[17] the harsh desert wind is Set, destroying the harvest, smothering the river. He tore his mother's womb at birth, and forced his way into the world through her side.[18] As Homer W. Smith relates,

> Set was an evil god, rather than a god of evil. In earliest times he had been credited with the murder of Osiris, and he forever typified the less admirable human traits. He was a prime liar and a breeder of mischief, and was forever destroying or attempting to destroy the good works of Osiris.[19]

Set had an abysmal temper, and was jealous of his brother Osiris, who was well loved over all the earth. When Set's wife seduced Osiris, it was the last straw Set needed to put an end to him. Set threw a party for the god of light and love, and put together a little game involving a chest (read "coffin") of exactly Osiris' proportions. When Osiris got inside, Set and his confederates slammed the door shut, soldered it with lead, and dumped it into the Nile. As if that wasn't enough, Set later found the chest, opened it, cut Osiris' body into fourteen pieces and dispersed them over the face of the earth. At last, Osiris' son Horus came of age, avenged his father, and vanquished Set, one wrathful god indeed.

In a similar vein, there is a particularly gruesome myth from ancient Babylon regarding Marduk's ascension to power. It seems the goddess Tiamat (primordial substance) and the god Apsu (matter) were the mother and father of all things. Eventually their grandchildren became so rowdy that it made life difficult for the divine parents. Apsu became so angry that he swore to slay his grandchildren just so that he could have a little peace. Tiamat tried to talk him out of it, but their first-born, Mummu, encouraged him. Word of the evil plan reached the younger gods, however, and they slew Apsu and maimed Mummu, yet they quailed at the thought of Tiamat's diabolical forces. They raised up a champion, Marduk, who made them promise to make him their sovereign should he succeed. They agreed, and Marduk disposed of Tiamat in a most gruesome battle, slitting her open "like a shellfish in two pieces. The one half he raised up and made the heavens as a shade therewith; he pulled the bolt, he posted a guard, he ordered them not to let her water escape."[20]

Zeus, too, was a younger god (of the Greek mythos) who challenged and destroyed his father, Kronos, freeing the Titans whom Uranus had bound in utter darkness, and becoming king of the gods in the same way as Marduk did (we will relate this story in detail later). Yet Zeus was little better behaved than his father, at times, and his wife, Hera, was often worse. She made a career out of destroying the lives of women who had the misfortune of being attractive to Zeus.

As we read these ancient mythologies, the moral ambiguity of the gods astounds us today. From the very beginning of Hindu cosmology, the horror is evident: "I am the food, food, food, and I am the eater, eater, eater...from food are born living beings. Those who are on the Earth live only by food and become themselves food."[21] Alain Daniélou comments on this passage,

> The Creator is a cruel god who made a world in which nothing can live but by destroying life through the killing of other living beings. Thus, no being can exist except by devouring other forms of life, whether vegetable or animal, and this is one of the fundamental aspects of created nature. Life in the world, both animal and human, is nothing but an interminable slaughter. To exist means to eat and to be eaten. Man is what he eats. All living beings feed on other beings and themselves become food for other beings....[22]

The king of the Vedic gods, Indra, is famous for his exploits on the battlefield and in the bedchamber, but like most polytheistic gods, he is also known for having a terrible temper. In a myth from the Jaiminiya Brahmana, his jealous nature is in evidence. It seems that all creation praised Indra, all except for a dolphin named Sarkara. Indra took notice and paid a visit to the neglectful water mammal. "I want you to praise me," Indra told him. But the dolphin told him, "No, I will not. I live in another world, under the sea. What have I to do with you? Here, this is how I praise you." And he spit water from his blowhole at the god.

So Indra commanded the forces of nature, and by means of rain and thunder he beached the dolphin, and then dried his skin with fierce winds. Sarkara the dolphin lay there on the beach, helpless, and said to himself, "This is no accident — this is Indra's doing. If I just praise him, perhaps he'll let me live." So he swallowed his pride and sang a song of praise to Indra. Then he raised his voice in prayer and asked to be returned to the water, then he sang his hymn again. Instead of going back into the water, he rose upon the hymn he sang into the heavens and became a constellation.[23]

Although this story has a happy ending, the cause of the dilemma for the poor, headstrong dolphin is Indra's adolescent demand to be admired. Wendy Doniger O'Flaherty ties this story to the traditional motif of the drought used for theological blackmail.[24] This story, while cruel, has a quality of cuteness to it lacking in most horrific narratives — then again, any horror story revolving around dolphins has an uphill battle not being cute.

There is nothing cute, however, about Agni, the god of fire. He appears upon the scene as a blaze that threatens the whole universe. The Satapatha Brahmana tells of the creation, when the primal god Prajapati made all creatures. He made the gods, too, and when he made Agni, the new god went a little power-mad and tried to burn up everything in sight. This caused all beings to flee from him in terror, which meant, of course, that no beings would sacrifice to him and he would have no food. So, ever the quick study, Agni paid a visit to human beings and made them a deal that they could not refuse.

"Let me live in you," he proposed, "and then you can bring me forth any time you please. Be my abode, and fire will ever be your servant. And if that is not enough, after you have died, if you burn your bodies, I will bring you back to life and give you a home in my abode." The humans said, "Sounds like you have a deal," and ever since human beings have been burned after death, so that they may live again.[25]

Other Vedic deities are notable for similarly threatening personalities. Varuna — supposedly the most moral of the Vedic deities — is also the god of snares, who entraps sinners; "Varuna seizes with his noose him who is seized with evil."[26] Varuna appears as "an evil-minded, terrifying god, from whom man wants to be delivered."[27] Like Varuna, Rudra (who would later become known as the great god Shiva) also carries a noose, and in later Hinduism, inherits the mantle of the sinner-snarer.[28]

Rudra is "the personification of anger,"[29] whose wrath is so great that even Indra quails in fear of him. The Taittiriya Upanishad says, "Out of fear of him the wind blows, out of fear the sun shines, out of fear fire and the king of heaven and death rush to their work"(2.8.1). The Atharva Veda says of him, "Rudra is the god that kills....(1.19.3). He is death...the demon...the cause of tears"(16.6.26).

This destructive element was bequeathed to Shiva, the god into whom Rudra developed, or more accurately, was subsumed. O'Flaherty writes, "In the Rig Veda, Rudra is invoked as a god of death: 'Do not slaughter our father or our mother.' In later metaphysical developments, death become less personal, and Shiva destroys the universe by fire at the end of each era, purifying it by sprinkling it with ashes."[30]

Like Indra above, Shiva is envious of honor not made to him. Because he is so uncouth, he was considered an outsider, and not given a portion of the sacrifice. In one myth, Daksha was a king and sage who invited the gods to a great sacrifice. Shiva was not invited, however, even though at Brahma's urging, he had given his own daughter, Sita, to Shiva in marriage. Daksha, in the Bhagavata Purana, says,

> "Against my own will...I gave my daughter to this unclean being, the destroyer of rites and social barriers, who teaches the sacred texts to men of low birth.... Like a madman, he haunts horrid cemeteries, surrounded with ghosts and evil spirits. He is naked, his hair in disorder. He laughs, he weeps, he smears himself with ashes and wears as his only ornament a necklace of skulls and human bones. He pretends he is 'of good omen,' but in reality he is 'of evil omen.' He is mad, adored by madmen, and reigns over the spirits of darkness. May this so-called sovereign, the last of the gods, never receive a part of the offerings of sacrifice."[31]

Sita, though not invited, came to the sacrifice anyway, and when she saw that no portion had been set aside for her husband, she committed suicide. Shiva, in retaliation for his loss, and because of the affront of not being given a portion, created a spirit called Birahandra who destroyed all those present, cut off the head of Daksha, and threw it into the fire. Shiva himself, however, pulled out the beard of the priest, squeezed out the eyes, and broke the teeth of two of the gods present.[32]

In a related myth, we learn how Rudra became the Lord of Beasts. It seems the gods divided up the beasts amongst themselves, yet gave none to Rudra. In retaliation, according to the Varaha Purana, Rudra broke the teeth of Pusan, put out Bhaga's eyes, and tore away both of Kratu's testicles. He gave them such a good beating that all the gods were rolling on the ground in agony, helpless and inarticulate—much like the animals they had horded for themselves. Eventually they recovered enough to crawl to Rudra's feet and make obeisance. Rudra wasn't done with them yet, and let loose with the verbal abuse next. "I was created before all these gods, and yet you deny me a share in the sacrifice? What do you think I am, chopped liver?"

That's a rather free paraphrase, obviously, but Rudra isn't done. "Because of this insult, I have denied these beasts the power of speech, and caused them to be malformed." They all cowered and tried to appease him. "Say, I have an idea," Rudra said. "How about I turn all of you into animals, and then I will be your king, for only then will your suffering cease." The gods, amazingly, agreed, and thereafter Rudra became known as Pasupati, the King of Beasts. He also gave Pusan's teeth back, restored Bhaga's sight, and re-grew Kratu's testicles.[33]

One of the most terrifying of Shiva's exploits involves his murder of the creator god, Brahma, found in the writings of the Kashmir Saivites. It seems that Brahma and Vishnu were arguing over which of them was the greatest. They both appealed to the scriptures to support their positions, but the scriptures seemed to support Rudra-Shiva as the supreme god. Neither of them were able to accept this verdict, because Rudra-Shiva was so revolting—in more ways than either of them could count. Brahma even laughed, "How in the world could the pure and dispassionate Ultimate Reality be over there making whoopee with his concubine, in plain view of all those deformed goblins that serve him? Ugh!"

But Om, the mystic sound that fills the universe, confirmed the testimony of the scriptures. "Behold," Om said, "Rudra-Shiva's consort is not partaking of something outside of herself—she embodies his divine essence. How could it be wrong to make love to yourself?" Just then a pillar of flame sprung up before Brahma and Vishnu, and levitating within it's pyric force was the three-eyed Rudra in all his iconographic glory, complete with trident, serpents, and crescent moon.

Brahma tried to appear unshaken. "I know who you really are, Rudra. I gave birth to you from out of my own forehead, remember? Take refuge in me, and I will protect you, my boy!" This only made Rudra-Shiva angrier and he magically conjured up a terrifying power-being he called, "Lord of Time and Death." "Go, and punish Bramha, and I will give to you a Kingdom—the cosmic graveyard where liberation is guaranteed." In a matter of mere seconds, the Lord of Time and Death flicked the head off of Brahma with his thumbnail. When he turned towards Vishnu, the blue god already had the hymnal open and was singing Rudra-Shiva's praises as the supreme god. The headless Brahma joined in as best he could, swaying his headless torso to the music. Rudra-Shiva smiled, because everyone loves to win an argument.[34]

Shiva's wrath is capricious as well. When Shiva's wife Parvati fashioned a luxurious flower garden, Shiva created a little boy to guard it. When some girls came in and picked the flowers without permission, the boy hid their clothes while they were bathing. The girls complained to Shiva, who had the boy impaled, apparently for simply doing his job.[35]

The mixture of adoration and horror that Shiva demands is evident in an ancient hymn of Basavanna: "Shiva, you have no mercy. Shiva, you have no heart. Why, why did you bring me to birth, wretch in this world, exile from the other?"[36]

Like Yahweh, Zeus, and so many other sky gods, Shiva is identified with the bull as his mount. The bull in many societies is the embodiment of sexual desire. The significance of Shiva's mount, according to Daniélou is that he rides — and is master of — his desire. "Shiva is the master of lust. He rides on the bull. With one glance of his third eye, the eye of higher perception, he reduces to ashes the Seducer-of-the-Mind, the god of love, who disturbs his meditation. Only those who have attained knowledge are the masters of their impulses, [and] can ride on the bull...."[37]

Those surrounding Shiva are likewise horrific. In the Matsya Purana, there is a story about the Matrkas, the wives of six sages who have been unjustly accused of adultery, and as a result are abandoned by their husbands. It is apparently a universal truth that "hell hath no fury like a woman scorned," for the Matrkas are eternally angry, and violent besides. Once, when Shiva was having trouble defeating a particularly nasty foe, he summoned the Matrkas to help him. The Matrkas are terrible in appearance, drinking the blood of demons. After a fierce battle, the Matrkas boast that they would now go on a bloody rampage, killing and eating every god, demon, and human being in the universe. Shiva warns them against this plan, but they blow him off and start eating. So Shiva calls Vishnu, who appears as his Man-Lion avatar, Narasimbha. Vishnu created a bunch of beautiful goddesses, whose ministrations distract the Matrkas from their wonton campaign of destruction.[38] This lesbian turn is not commented upon, but the Matrkas asked for a boon since they did actually help Shiva. He charged them with the duty of tormenting children until they are sixteen years of age, and granted them an eternally violent nature—which, apparently, pleased them.[39]

Hinduism is full of similarly wrathful goddesses. Devi, the Great Goddess, is a formidable warrior and is often called upon when danger threatens the universe. She usually appears peaceful and beneficent, but once she gets on the battlefield, her bloodlust escalates and she becomes a mindless killing machine, able to split herself into several beings, all attacking in concert. Once the taste of blood was in her mouth, however, she was hard to stop. She could always be counted upon to help the gods out of a jam, but she also had a tendency to get carried away and become a threat to the stability of the universe in her own right.[40]

Once, in the Devi Bhagavata Purana, the gods ask Devi to show her universal form. She obliged, much to the gods' horror. She appeared as having a thousand heads, eyes, and feet. "Her entire body blazes with fierce, destructive flames, and her teeth make horrible grinding noises. Her eyes blaze with flames brighter than millions of suns, and the gods tremble as they see her consume the universes."[41] The gods ask her to please assume her gentle form again, which she does, much to their relief.

Another of the great goddesses is Durga, who rides a lion, and who, like Devi (of whom she is a form) chiefly attacks demons who threaten the worlds. She is called sleep, hunger, shadow, thirst, and delusion.[42]

Her origin is told in the myth of the defeat of Mahisa, a very powerful demon, who had raised his *tapas* (spiritual power) by means of great austerities. So great was his power that he was granted the power to be invincible to any man. So Mahisa went out and challenged every god to battle—and won. He stole their thrones along with their pride. Finally, the defeated gods gathered together and vented their rage at Mahisa's conquering spree. They focused their spiritual energies, and a great white ball of light hovered in the air. Eventually, the light coalesced into a being—a beautiful woman. Her body possessed parts of all those male gods that had pooled their energies. Durga—for that was what they called her—cast back her head and roared, and the earth quaked in response. Mahisa would soon quake himself, for though no man could defeat him, no one said anything about a woman.[43]

Durga rivals Shiva for revolting devotional practices. Her followers made offerings of their own flesh and blood, and she is known for her taste for intoxicating drink, for meat, and for blood.[44]

The most famous and terrifying of Devi's forms is Kali. Kali appears in the Linga Purana when Shiva asks his wife Parvati to destroy the demon Daruka, who also has the good fortune of only being able to be defeated by a woman. Parvati enters Shiva's body, and inhabiting the poison stored in his neck, bursts forth as Kali, the most ferocious and nefarious of the goddesses.[45] Kali, typically, goes overboard, and Shiva has to intervene before the world is destroyed. The goddesses seem to be somewhat inter-changeable, as even Sita can evoke and transform herself into Kali, as she does in the Ramayana.

The Kali Tantra describes Kali in her iconic form: she is typically depicted standing on a corpse (which is sometimes clearly Shiva!). In her four arms she holds a sword and a severed head. Her remaining arms display mudras representing the removing of fear and the granting of favors. She is naked, sky-clad—both terrible and glorious to behold. Her tongue is usually hanging out of her mouth and of an obscene length, and her neck is adorned with a garland of severed heads.[46]

Kali hangs about in battlefields, getting drunk on the blood of her slain, or in cremation grounds, sitting on corpses surrounded by jackals and goblins.[47] Her most famous appearances occur in the Devi Mahatmya, where it is told that Durga was battling two vicious demons, Canda and Munda. The demons marched toward her with weapons drawn. Durga's fury mounted, and her face turned jet black. Suddenly from her forehead sprung another goddess, Kali, who was black as midnight. She roared and lunged at the demons, whom she tore to shreds with her bare hands.

Later, Durga summoned her against another demon, Raktabija, who had the power to multiply himself whenever a drop of his own blood touched the earth.

Durga discovered that in wounding Raktabija, she had only made things worse, as there continued to be so many more of him! But Kali knew what to do—she grabbed each Raktabija and sucked his blood dry, casting the drained corpses onto a pile.[48]

On their own, both Shiva and Kali can be devastating, and together, they spur one another to disaster. In one South Indian tale, the two had a dance contest that nearly destroyed the world.[49] Of her the poet Ramprasad wrote with some hint of despair,

Can mercy be found in the heart
of her who was born of the stone?
Were she not merciless,
would she kick the breast of her lord?
Men call you merciful,
but there is no trace of mercy in you, Mother.
You have cut off the heads of the children of others,
and these you wear as a garland around your neck.
It matters not how much I call you,
"Mother, Mother."
You hear me, but you will not listen.[50]

Other horrific goddesses include Nirrti, a sinister figure embodying misery, disease, and death, who was only invoked in the Rig Veda in order to be told to go away! She was "the wife of Sin...: Her sons are Death, Fear, and Terror."[51] Another was known as the Crane-headed goddess, who presided over all the subtle forms of killing. She was the goddess of black magic and of poisons. According to Daniélou, she "rules over the subtle perception which make us feel at a distance the death or misery of those we know. She incites men to torture one another. She revels in suffering."[52]

Shiva was not the only of the later great gods who was fiercesome; even the normally benign Vishnu has had his share of horrific forms, such as the Man-Lion, the Nrsimha Avatara. The tale is told of a pious boy, Prahlada, whose evil father, the king, was in no way pleased about his son's religious leanings, and punished him mercilessly. Eventually the king decided that it would be best to kill the child, rather than to suffer his devotional proclivities. Miraculously, however, the boy, sitting in meditation, was protected, and no harm could come to him. The king was possessed of a genie, who had promised him that no god, animal, demon, or human being could harm him. To rescue Prahlada, Vishnu became half-man, half-lion, and tore out the entrails of the genie.[53] This aspect of Vishnu only makes rare appearances, but it is important as a token towards balance between the competing natures of Shiva and Vishnu.

Of wrath, the gods of Hinduism have no lack, and are some of the most horrific deities in the history of religion. It is important to note however, that the wrath of the great gods is not, by and large, directed at human beings, but at demonic beings who threaten the universal order. When human beings do become victims it is usually because they were in the wrong place at the wrong time. Unlike the wrath of Yahweh, which we shall consider in the next section, the Hindu gods' wrath isn't personal and is rarely directed at people.

The God of Wrath
in the Abrahamic Traditions

Even a cursory reading of the Hebrew scriptures reveals an undeniable fact: the God of the Hebrews gets angry—and not, typically, at demons, but primarily at people. The Abrahamic traditions usually speak of this fact as justifiable. God gets angry at people for good reasons, or so the scriptures relate. The inhabitants of Sodom and Gomorrah were wicked, as were the people of the whole Earth prior to the flood; the people of Israel were fickle, worshipping the gods of their neighbors; the people of Israel expected God's anger to be poured out upon their enemies (which they perceived as justifiable). But a closer reading betrays this simplistic assumption. The anger of the Abrahamic God is frequently out of proportion to the wrongs committed, and often seems mean-spirited and arbitrary, as we shall see.

Baudler points out that, "In the oldest biblical texts, evil is a dimension of God."[54] He goes on to cite the story of Moses (Exodus 4-12), who, having resisted Yahweh's command to lead the people of Israel out of Egypt, finally gave in and set off with his wife and his brother, Aaron. Inexplicably, God entered their camp by night and tried to kill Moses. God's blood thirst was appeased in a moment of intuitive genius, when Moses' wife Zipporah decided that cutting off her son's foreskin as a bloody sacrifice might appease the deity.

Georg Baudler comments, "Obviously, Yahweh has a demonic character here.... Zipporah...takes a flint, cuts off her son's foreskin and touches Moses' legs with it to mark him a 'bride-groom of blood,' a hero who has fought against the power of chaos, shedding his blood and thus earning a place at the sacred wedding."[55] This betrays the early Hebrew opinion that their God can be appeased in much the same way as the gods of their neighbors: by the shedding of blood. By blood, the angel of death (which, by the way, is not a demon, but God's angel) knew to pass over the houses of the Israelites; and by sacrifices of blood were the people of Israel cleansed of their sin. Blood was, throughout the biblical record, of utmost power and importance.

This similarity of Yahweh to the gods of Israel's neighbors is evidenced also by the imagery of the earliest Hebrew scriptures, where God was given very bull-like attributes. Baudler suggests that the golden calf was not "another god" but an attempt by the Israelites to put into an image their perception of Yahweh. Bull imagery also appeared repeatedly in the Levitical descriptions of the temple, and especially on the ark of the covenant (the horns of the mercy seat, etc.). In 1 Kings 12:28ff Yahweh is venerated again in the form of a bull.[56] The prophet Balaam, in Numbers 23-24 said, "God...is like the wild ox's horns to him. He feeds on the carcasses of his enemies, and he breaks their bones in pieces." Baudler writes,

> Wherever the fury and anger of Yahweh is leveled against the enemies of Israel, the "bull El" appears, capricious, unpredictable, and wild. He howls, he slashes with a blade, he walks in flames, he strikes, hunts down, grabs, and strangles. He stalks like a panther; he assaults like a bear; he lacerates like a lion. He splits the earth, makes it tremble, frightens the sun and the moon who hide from him. He pelts with hail, shatters people like earthenware, and casts the fleeing kings of Sodom and Gomorrah into pits of pitch. He is a maiming rock, he demands banishment and impalement, he appears as one who has trodden in the winepress and his garments are red from the blood of the people he has trampled in his wrath (Isaiah 63:2ff).[57]

God's wrath was by no means reserved for Israel's enemies, however. In many cases it was leveled against Israel herself. "If in spite of this, you do not obey me," warned God in Leviticus 26:27-30, "then I will act with wrathful hostility against you; and I even I, will punish you seven times for your sins. Further, you shall eat the flesh of your sons and the flesh of your daughters you shall eat. And then I will destroy your high places and cut down your incense alters...for my soul shall abhor you.

In Deuteronomy 28:63-68, we find that God's violence is not restricted to the physical, but promises psychological violence as well:

> As the Lord delighted over you to prosper you...so the Lord will delight over you to make you perish and destroy you; and

you shall be torn from the land... And among the nations you shall find no rest, and there shall be no resting place for the sole of your foot; but there the Lord will give you a trembling heart, failing of eyes, and despair of soul. So your life shall hang in doubt before you; and you shall be in dread night and day, and shall have no assurance of your life. In the morning you shall say, "Would that it were evening!" And at evening you shall say, "Would that it were morning!" because of the dread of your heart....

Sometimes God's wrath is capricious. In Leviticus 10:1-2, Nadab and Abihu, the sons of Aaron, offered up incense in a way that was not "approved" of by God, and "a fire came out from the presence of the Lord and consumed them, and they died before the Lord."

In 2 Samuel 6:6-8, we read that when David and his men were transporting the ark back to Israel, the oxen stumbled. In order that the ark would not fall to the ground, "Uzzah reached out toward the ark of God, and took hold of it, for the oxen nearly upset it. And the anger of the Lord burned against Uzzah, and God struck him down there for his irreverence; and he died by the ark of God." An interesting addendum to this incident is the fact that David himself felt that this was unjust, and became angry at God for his childish outburst towards someone who was only trying to help.

Initially, the God revealed in the Christian scriptures appears more benign, if more complex; a deity who "sends the rain upon the just and unjust alike" and has more affinity for the sinners than the self-righteous saints. But a closer inspection reveals a God guilty of divine child abuse. In the Christian tradition the cruel test Yahweh puts to Abraham — to sacrifice his only son — is carried through. It is the sacrifice of Jesus — God's only child — that appeases God's blood thirst and wins for the elect a reprieve from God's temporal — and eternal — wrath.

This theory of atonement has its roots in Paul's epistles and the Epistle to the Hebrews, and is most fully articulated in the

Christian tradition by St. Anselm. In short, Anselm saw God as a medieval feudal lord, whose serfs, by disobeying him, have besmirched his honor. Because God's honor has been offended, he cannot look upon humanity, let alone embrace them. The barrier to communion between God and humanity therefore lies in God, who must save face before "he" can begin to really forgive. Jesus, in coming as the "suffering servant," succeeded in living a full human life without sin, therefore restoring God's honor. In return, God granted Jesus the "boon" of eternal life. Since Jesus is God, he does not need this gift, and passes it along to the Church to mete out in the sacraments.

Because grace is a commodity that can change hands, this is sometimes referred to as the "Commercial" theory of the atonement.

Calvin's theory of Divine Justice is similar to it. The barrier to communion between humans and God is once more in God, who cannot consort with convicted criminals, for that is what humans are, under the Mosaic Law. According to this divine law of the universe, which even God cannot contradict, all sin must be punished by the shedding of blood. In the crucifixion, Jesus bore in his person the accumulated wrath of God towards all sinners, past, present, and future.

Feminist theologians have pointed out that the model of Christ as the "suffering servant" is the primary force in shaping women's acceptance of abuse. According to Joanne Carlson Brown and Carole Bohn, "the central image of Christ on the cross...communicates the message that suffering is redemptive. If the best person who ever lived gave his life for others, then, to be of value we should likewise sacrifice ourselves. Any sense that we have a right to care for our own needs is in conflict with being a faithful follower of Jesus."[58]

The greatest irony of the Commercial and Justice theories is the implication that God demands of "his" followers a discipline that "he" is not willing to practice "himself:" the discipline of forgiveness without retribution. Even though Jesus tells us that we should forgive one another "seventy times seven times" (Matthew 18:21-22; Luke 17:3-4), yet the author of the Epistle to the Hebrews insists that "without the shedding of blood there is no forgiveness" (9:22).

According to the Justice theory, God's wrath cannot simply be set aside, but must make some person suffer—even if it is an innocent person. God the "Father" must satisfy "his" urge towards violence before "he" is willing to forgive, in direct opposition to Jesus' own instructions to us. One must ask, if we are to "be perfect even as your Father in heaven is perfect" (Matthew 5:48) how is it that behavior is required of us that God is not capable—or not willing—to model?

This odd dichotomy is even celebrated by St. Paul in his Epistle to the Romans:

Do not repay anyone evil for evil, but take thought for what is noble in the sight of all.... Beloved, never avenge yourselves, but leave room for the wrath of God; for it is written, "Vengeance is mine, I will repay, says the Lord." No, "if your enemies are hungry, feed them; if they are thirsty, give them something to drink; for by doing this you will heap burning coals on their heads." Do not be overcome by evil, but overcome evil with good (12:14-21 NRSV).

The mental image of St. Paul chuckling over the idea of kindness being experienced as "burning coals" makes one wonder if Paul has missed the very point he is trying to drive home.

The Christian concept of God has lost none of the Jewish God's capriciousness. In the fifth chapter of Acts the story is related about Ananias and Sapphira, a married couple in the church at Jerusalem who sold a piece of property in order to make a donation to the church. Keeping some of the money for themselves, they lied to the apostles and said that the offering they were giving was the whole amount gained from the sale. Instead of using this as an experience by which the deceitful couple might learn from their mistake and make wiser choices in the future, God's "justice" was swift:

> "Ananias," Peter asked, "why has Satan filled your heart to lie to the Holy Spirit and to keep back part of the proceeds of the land? ...You did not lie to us but to God!" Now when Ananias heard these words, he fell down and died. And great fear seized all who heard of it. ...After an interval of about three hours his wife came in, not knowing what had happened. Peter said to her, "Tell me whether you and your husband sold the land for such and such a price." And she said, "Yes, that was the price." Then Peter said to her, "How is it that you have agreed together to put the Spirit of the Lord to the test? Look, the feet of those who have buried your husband are at the door, and they will carry you out." Immediately she fell down at his feet and died. When the young men came in they found her dead, so they carried her out and buried her beside her husband. And great fear seized the whole church and all who heard of these things (3-11 NRSV).

In the Koran, we see the same sort of moral ambivalence in Allah. Though Allah makes it plain that "he" is not above bloodshed (17:16, 19:98), the real relish and violence is reserved for more eschatological scenarios. Like Christianity, in which the Trinitarian concept of God became more paradoxical and difficult, Islam codified the Hebrew monotheistic impulse, creating an image of Allah that is both merciful and terrible. According to Baudler,

> In Islam, the ancient Semitic form Il, El, Al for God becomes "Allah." Like El-Yahweh, the protective and paternal/maternal God "I-am-here," Allah is kind and merciful. All suras of the

Koran (except for Sura 9) begin "In the name of Allah, the merciful, the compassionate." His mercifulness includes everything, it "knows no limit" (Sura 7:156). His original character as bull has metamorphosed into grandeur, majesty, and omnipotence. And yet, he has not lost his temperamental tendencies. In contrast to Yahweh, and even more so to the Abba Jesus, who "is love" (John 1:14-16), his mercy does not include meekness and charity. He is above such emotions. His "rahma" (Mercy) is only an "in'am" (gift), and "ifdal" and "ihsam" (favor and blessing). Love, in the sense of an emotional bond, does not occur in the Koran. In this sense, Allah has adopted little of the features of Baal and the mother-goddess and even less of Yahweh and the Abba Jesus. He remains much more an Al, Il, El: the original bull, pushing forward with power and might.[59]

As in most societies, human beings feel that as God behaves, so they are given license to behave. The current world-wide terrorist crisis, where Muslim extremists feel justified in taking the lives of innocents in the name of God, is a prime example of this impulse. If Allah promises in the Koran to smite the unbeliever, then why not become the hand of Allah and speed the process along? The grim justice of Allah is chilling in the words of Ayatollah Khomeini:

> If the punitive laws of Islam were applied for only one year, all the devastating injustices would be uprooted. Misdeeds must be punished by the law of retaliation: cut off the hands of the thief; kill the murderer; flog the adulterous woman or man. Your concerns, your "humanitarian" scruples are more childish than reasonable. Under the terms of Koranic law, any judge fulfilling the seven requirements [that he have reached puberty, be a believer, know the Koranic laws perfectly, be just; and not be affected by amnesia, or be a bastard, or be of

the female sex] is qualified to be a judge in any type of case. He can thus judge and dispose of twenty trials in a single day, whereas the Occidental justice might take years to argue them out.[60]

Where the God of Wrath has been lifted up to the exclusion of a god of mercy or compassion, violence and devastation have invariably followed, especially when God's followers have felt that their mission has been "righteous." Neither the slaughter of Israel's neighbors, the Crusades, the Christian Inquisition, the Islamic jihads, nor the "global war on terror" would have been possible without a dominant theology of Wrath.

"...And lead us not into temptation."

Matthew 6:13

"God sent them a delusion,
that they should believe a lie..."

2 Thessalonians 2:11

Chapter Three

The Gods of Betrayal

As a teenager, I can remember long and sleepless nights, plagued by the just-dawning glimmers of my existential plight. God had placed me in a world I could not control, in a body wracked by feelings and urges clearly beyond my power to harness, handed me an impossible list of demands to fulfill, and then dangled me over the pit of Hell, threatening to drop me should I fail.

The insomnia came not so much from the threat of hellfire, but from the despair of feeling trapped by the situation. Success seemed an unreachable ideal, and the specter of my own looming death shouted that there was no escape from it. I would die, and I would fail. And this terrible knowledge mocked me without mercy as the clock ticked off the hours in the dark. And it was then, in the wee hours of my adolescent dark night that the horrid truth occurred to me: God had intentionally set me up. God had demanded my worship and devotion and service, and more than this, my love and trust, and then turned around and betrayed me.

Wrath I could handle—I could bear my father's wrath because I trusted that beneath it all, he really did love me and want the best for me. And until I hit adolescence, I believed the same about God. But as I agonized about the impossible situation God had personally placed me in, I trusted him no longer. I imagined myself to be a worm in a coffee can God was poking at for the cruel joy of watching me squirm.

As the following stories reveal, I was not alone in my feelings of betrayal. Countless others before me have found their gods to be equally deceptive, willfully throwing people into situations ranging from mischief to damnation, all to achieve their own inscrutable ends. Humans are helpless to divine the motives of their gods once the almighty ones elect to deceive them. We are like caged animals, our fate subject to the capricious whims of the untrustworthy Divine.

Betrayal in Polytheistic Traditions

One of the earliest examples of this is the nearly ubiquitous figure of the trickster. Not yet fully a god, the trickster was nevertheless a character of mythic proportions whose mischievous antics—for good or ill—held consequential import for the world. In many native mythologies, it was the trickster in the form of an Old Man, a Coyote, a Raven, or a Great Hare who succeeded in salvaging an habitable earth out of a bit of mud scraped from the bottom of the oceans. Joseph Campbell described its widespread influence:

> In Polynesia, Maui is the trickster... Br'er Rabbit has taught us something of his African form, where he is also Anansi, the spider. Among the Greeks he was Hermes (Mercury), the shape-shifter and master of the way to the land of the dead, as well as Prometheus, the fire-bringer. In Germanic myth he appeared as the mischief-maker, Loki, whose very character was fire and who, at the time of Ragnarök, the Twilight of the Gods, will be the leader of the hosts of Hel.[1]

One notable trickster is found in Yoruban myth by the name of Eshu, who is the gatekeeper of the abode of the gods, constantly confusing people with his trickery.[2] Eshu gained his fame by an act of deicide, when he dropped a boulder onto the god Orisha's house. "Orisha was crushed and, with the splinters of his house, was scattered and flew in all directions. Thus fragments of the divine spirit can be found in many places, in all living beings, even in the winds and rivers. That is why there are now 401 Orishas or gods."[3]

Eshu does not act on his own—he is an agent of the Supreme God, Olodumare. Eshu is sent forth from the court of the great God to try people, to see what they are really made of. Eshu travels the world over, spying on people, and setting people against one another to see what they will do. Sometimes his actions are in the interest of justice, to punish people or to even the score between two parties. He is not only the bringer of misery, however. For those who are truly good, he brings reward, and is often invoked by barren women in hope of becoming pregnant. Most traditional homes have an idol of Eshu, more out of fear of his capricious actions than out of love for him.[4]

Similar figures are common the world over. Among the plains people of North America, the trickster was known as Iktomi, who caused so much strife between the sun and the moon that he was banished.[5] Amongst the Sonhai people of Northern Africa, he was known as Irke. They called him both "Our Master" and "the Deceiver."[6] In its primitive form, the trickster is a stroke of genius, for, as among the Yorubans, it betrays the intuition that "good and evil spring forth from the same spirit at different times and for different reasons," in the same way as it does for normal people, because "there must be a balance in our views of people and in our beliefs in the gods."[7]

In later polytheism, the figure of the trickster underwent a transformation. As Leonard Biallas explains,

This mythic figure in most ancient form serves as a link between the heavens and earth, a channel to the gods. He bestows on humans gifts of their material and spiritual heritage and makes them aware of their godlike knowledge and their responsibilities to civilization. As cultures become more sophisticated, the trickster's role undergoes a transformation. No longer is he pictured as one who helped shape creation and furnish order; on the contrary he comes to stand for the principle of disorder, irrationality, and arbitrariness. This second form is familiar to us: the trickster as serpent, as spoiler, who plays a variety of mean tricks on the world, and thus introduces disorder.[8]

Nowhere is this shift more obvious than in the Greek myth of Prometheus, where both interpretations of the trickster are in evidence. Prometheus began his career as humanity's best friend. He fashioned us out of clay, and bestowed upon us the gifts of mathematics, metal-working, architecture, a calendar, writing, and most problematical of all, fire.[9]

As Michael Macrone tells it,

These achievements only made Zeus more jealous. The last straw was [Prometheus'] attempt to deprive Zeus of his due from a burnt offering. Prometheus covered up the useless bones in a promising looking lump of fat, hid the good bits under the beast's stomach (the gods didn't go for stomachs), and invited Zeus to choose his share.

Zeus was fooled, and mighty unhappy about it. To forestall future shenanigans, the god deprived [humankind] of fire, prompting Prometheus to pull his most heroic and most foolish caper. He stole up to Mount Olympus and, when no one was looking, bottled up enough fire in the hollow of a fennel stalk to get things burning again back on earth.[10]

Prometheus was the hero who stood up to the gods and called them on their transgressions, and he paid for his antics by being tied to a column and having an eagle eat out his liver. This would be bad enough, except that his liver grew back every night so that every day there was another feast for the eagle, day after day, forever. But amazingly, Zeus' wrath was not exhausted by this sentence—humanity suffered as well: as punishment for the human race, Zeus created woman, "through whose folly all kinds of plagues were let loose upon the earth,"[11] as evidenced in the myth of Pandora's box.

The fire-god Hephaestus created Pandora, and all the other gods helped by bestowing on her beauty, charm, domestic talents, the gift of flattery, and a deceptive nature.

Zeus released her upon the earth, and Hermes arranged for her to meet the unsuspecting Epimetheus, the brother of Prometheus. Prometheus had warned his brother that the gods might try something like this, but Epimetheus simply could not resist her, and married her immediately. (One has to wonder how he knew to do this, since there were no women on the earth up until that point.)

Previous to this, Zeus had sent Epimetheus another gift, a box, which he was told never to open. At least this temptation Epimetheus was able to resist, but alas, Pandora could not. Once she was told about the mysterious box, she took the first opportunity to open it, and all the evils of the world rushed out.[12]

While Prometheus is more than human, he is less than a god. The divine trickster in Greek myth is perhaps best represented by Hermes, who started out his life in a very tricky manner. The same day he was born he picked up his walking stick and journeyed to Thessaly, where Apollo, his half-brother, was working in the fields herding sheep. When Apollo wasn't looking, Hermes stole a significant number of the herd, and hid them in a nearby cave.

Somehow, Apollo figured out who had done it (even though he had not yet even met his younger brother), and angrily confronted Hermes' mother. She called his accusations nonsense, for Hermes was just a newborn baby, and besides, here he was, sleeping in his crib. Apollo wasn't fooled by Hermes' quick-footed tomfoolery, and he took the infant from the crib and presented his grievance to their father, Zeus. There, Hermes admitted his crime and returned the stolen animals. Far from being angry, Zeus was delighted by his little one's mischievous spunk and speedy nature, and made him his personal messenger.[13]

Trickery on the part of the gods is far from unusual. By hook or by crook, it seems that the gods always get their way. In the Iliad, Zeus sends a dream to trick Agamemnon into attacking without Achilles, and "even so the Greeks get the better of the fighting...[since Zeus] intervenes to guarantee Trojan success."[14] At the funeral games to honor Patroclus, Odysseus is racing Ajax. Ajax is ahead, so Odysseus prays to Athena, "who makes Ajax slip on some cow manure. With mingled good humor and irritability, Ajax says, 'O popoi! I was tripped up by that goddess who has always stood by Odysseus and looks after him like a mother!' And all the Greeks laugh."[15]

These two examples come from the Iliad and the Odyssey, in which Homer takes different approaches to the deception of the gods. As Lloyd-Jones points out, in the Odyssey, "the gods do not themselves put wrong ideas into men's minds, but men blame the gods for their own foolish actions. In the Iliad once the gods have determined to destroy a man they see to it that he decides disastrously."[16]

In Hesiod we find the story of Eros, who "loosens the limbs and damages the mind.... Eros was...an emotional terrorist, inflicting strange, uncontrollable feelings and inspiring endless cruelties."[17] This may say more about the Greeks' fear of emotions than anything else, but nonetheless, Eros was seen as a very dangerous character, determined to get men and gods alike out of their right minds, crazed with love doomed to fail. He was prone to tantrums (once breaking one of Zeus' thunderbolts into bits), and had as his weapons twin arrows of gold and lead. Macrone explains, "The golden arrows would inflame their target's passions, sometimes resulting in happiness and sometimes in disaster. The leaden arrows, however, were just plain bad, since they inspired only disgust and hatred. You may have noticed that [Eros] tends to shoot these arrows in tandem: as soon as you're hit by a golden one, he aims a leaden arrow at the object of your fancy."[18]

Perhaps the greatest betrayal of all, however, is the betrayal of one's children, and examples of divine child abuse are common, and nowhere better exemplified than in the Greek tales of Uranus and Kronos. In one myth, Mother Earth (Gaea) brought forth from her own abundance Father Sky, otherwise known as Uranus. Uranus enveloped her round about, and provided real estate for Olympia, the celestial home of the gods. Gaea and Uranus then married, and from their union came the Titans. First came the three giants. These wondrous beings had a hundred hands each, and fifty heads, and fifty arms. Next they gave birth to three Cyclops. Uranus hated his children, for he felt threatened by their power. One by one, he bound them fast and cast them deep into their mother, the Earth. Each of them fell for nine days, finally crashing to the ground in the underworld of Tarturus.

Gaea loved her children and was furious at Uranus for his betrayal. So, in secret she met with her sons and told them she wanted them to take revenge on their father. They were all scared of Uranus, but Kronos, the youngest of the Titans, agreed. So Gaea gave Kronos a scythe made of stone, and told him what to do. When Uranus laid down beside the waters to sleep with Gaea, Kronos leaped out of hiding and castrated his father. He threw Uranus' severed member into the water and declared Uranus' reign ended. "And now shall I reign in your place," he added.

But Kronos proved just as frightened of his brothers, the Giants and the Cyclopes, and also kept them imprisoned. Gaea felt betrayed, and once again plotted to liberate the other Titans. She prophesied that one day Kronos' own son would overthrow him, just as he had done his father. She took great joy in relating this prophesy, and it ate away at Kronos' dreams.

Kronos and his wife Rhea had a daughter named Hestia, and when Kronos first laid eyes upon her, all he could hear were the echoes of Gaea's prophesy. Without even bothering to discover the gender of the child, he ate her whole. He swallowed with satisfaction, thinking that he had cheated fate. Rhea had three more children, Demeter, Hera, Hades, and Poseidon, and Kronos swallowed each one of them as soon as they were presented to him.

When Zeus was born, Rhea had wised up to her husband's ways, and slipped Kronos a stone wrapped in swaddling clothes, while stealing the baby Zeus away to be raised by her own mother, Gaea. Kronos gobbled up the stone, and Zeus grew to full god-hood. When the time was ripe, he enlisted the aid of his uncles, the Giants and the Cyclopes, freed them, and defeated Kronos. Zeus took the throne, and though he was not as cruel to his own children, he retained his share of Kronos' demonic character.[19]

The Gods of
Betrayal in Hinduism

Throughout her mythical life, Hinduism's gods have had a deceptive character, deluding humans to keep them in check, and deceiving demons in order to defeat them. And although the Satapatha Brahmana says the "gods relinquished untruth, and the demons relinquished truth,"[20] the stories below call this statement into question.

It is due to the gods' deception that the Hindu demons are demons in the first place. In addition to the story related in Chapter One (in which the original demons steal the elixir of immortality, and thus become the gods), there are many other similar tales. In the Satapatha Brahmana, we read that, "The gods...began to perform the sacrifice, and each time the demons came where they were preparing it the gods snatched up the sacrifice and began doing something else. And the demons went away, thinking, 'It is something else they are doing.' Then the gods completed the sacrifice and they prevailed, and the demons came to naught."[21]

In another myth, the demons had been beaten in battle by the gods, and they took refuge with the guru Maya (which means "delusion"), who built them three cities. The demons lived in those three cities, and set about to destroy the world. Shiva shot the demons with his arrow, and they fell down lifeless. Maya threw them into a magic well, where they were revived. Shiva was worried, but Vishnu had a plan: he and Brahma entered the city disguised as cattle, and drank up the elixir of immortality in the magic well, after which Shiva was able to destroy the cities.[22]

Demons are not the only targets of the gods' trickery—human beings run afoul of them as well. According to the Jaiminiya Brahmana,

> The gods and demons were striving against each other. The gods created a thunderbolt, sharp as a razor, that was man. They hurled this at the demons, and it scattered the demons, but then it turned back to the gods. The gods were afraid of it, and so they took it and broke it into three pieces. Then they saw that the divinities had entered into this man in the form of hymns. They said, "When this man has lived in the world with merit, he will follow us by means of sacrifices and good deeds and asceticism. Let us therefore act so that he will not follow us. Let us put evil in him." They put evil in him: sleep, laziness, anger, hunger, love of dice, desire for women. These are the evils that assail a man in this world.
>
> Then they enjoined Agni in this world. "Agni, if anyone escapes evil and aspires to do good things in this world, try to ruin him." And they enjoined Vayu in the intermediate air in the same way, and the sun in the sky.[23]

The reasons for the gods wanting humans to be evil goes back to our previous discussions of the nature of evil in Hinduism in Chapter One. In the myth above, the three sparks are probably the three Vedas, which teach humankind about righteousness. But humankind's righteousness, in the period that this brahmana was written, threatens the power of the gods, and must be curtailed.

Occurring again and again in Hindu mythology is the notion that heresies arise as the result of the gods' will. This is not surprising due to the astounding number of competing sects in Hinduism's history, and since all is God, how could it be that a heresy could arise that was not of God's design? God's design is not always benevolent: it is often meant to deceive and lead people – and demons – into delusion.

Why do this? The Saiva Siddhantas teach that God casts "his" illusion over humanity in order to make them dependent upon "him," to inspire devotion, but also to lead potentially powerful spiritual beings astray, and so to nullify the threat they pose to the gods' own power. The gods often send their maya to delude humans and demons. Maya, "illusion" is "that which impels individuals into self-centered, egotistical actions. Maya is the sense of ego, personal identity, and individuality which clouds the underlying unity of reality and masks one's essential identity with Brahman or some exalted being such as Vishnu, Shiva, or Durga."[24]

In the Devi Purana we read about a demon named Ghora, who tried to evict the gods from heaven, to take it for himself. Indra, instructed by Brahma, sent Narada to trick Ghora and his family into believing a false teaching, so that all his people would lose their power. Narada approached Ghora and told him, "The most efficacious method of pleasing the gods is by your own enjoyment of sensuality. All the gods love pleasure. Look at Shiva, for instance – he took all the Pine Forest sages' wives to his own bed, and he is the most enlightened being there is."

So Ghora abandoned the truth and embraced Narada's heresy. He took the wives of others to his own bed, and forsook his own mate. Knowing she was feeling neglected and was therefore vulnerable, Narada counseled Ghora's wife to embrace the heresy of the Jains. For the master stroke, Narada convinced Ghora to try to bed Shiva's wife, Parvati. As soon as he approached her, however, she slew him instantly.[25]

The most notorious of the "divine deceptions," however, in this writer's estimation, is the Buddha incarnation of Vishnu. The Bhagavata Purana "predicts": "When the Kali Age has begun, in order to delude the enemies of the gods, Vishnu will be born as the Buddha, son of Ajhana.... When the enemies of the gods come to know the Vedic rites and begin to oppress people, then he will assume an attractive and deluding form and teach adharma to the demons in the three invisible cities made by Maya, making them heretics.... With words he will delude those who are not deserving of the sacrifice."[26]

The prophesy is "fulfilled" in the Shiva Purana, which says that the demons who lived in the Triple city had attained great spiritual power through their ascetic practices. Their power was so great that they burned the gods themselves! So Indra and the other gods carried their complaint to Shiva, saying, "Those demons have got to go! They are more powerful than we are, they are stealing the sacrifices, and are upsetting the balance of the universe!" Shiva was sympathetic, but sadly told them, "The king of the Triple City is a devotee of mine, and a good man. I cannot destroy his city."

The gods were crestfallen, but Vishnu stepped up and declared, "The demons are righteous, and therefore we cannot touch them. Even when they sin, they pray to Shiva and are forgiven. So, for the sake of all the gods, I will create an obstacle to their righteousness, so that the Triple City can be destroyed."

Vishnu was therefore born as the Buddha, a teacher of falsehood, in order to destroy the demons, and lead them astray from the true doctrine. At first, no one listened to him, but he told Narada to pretend to convert. When the King of the demons saw that Narada had converted, he submitted and became a Buddhist monk. The Buddha mocked the true teachings of the Brahmins, and all the demons followed suit. Eventually women came to be initiated. When Vishnu saw that he had corrupted even the women, he knew his job was done. The gods approached Shiva and informed him that the demons had all converted to Buddhism, and had abandoned the worship of the gods. Even the king had converted. When he heard this, Shiva razed the Triple City to the ground with fire. Only Maya survived.[27]

This horrendous assimilation of Buddhism into orthodox Hinduism is shocking, but understandable considering the sectarian skirmishes of the early Bhaktic Hindu period. In the Garuda Purana, a similar tale is told regarding the Jains: "During the battle between gods and demons, the gods were defeated and sought refuge with the Lord; he became the son of Suddhodana, the very form of Mayamoha, and deluded the demons, who became Buddhists and abandoned the Vedas. Then he became an Arhat (Jain) and made others into Arhats, and so the heretics came into being."[28]

Charles Coleman called Vishnu's behavior in these myths "More demoniacal than divine, and more in accordance with the character of a minister of evil, than of the preserving deity of the universe."[29]

The God of Betrayal
in the Abrahamic Religions

The God of Betrayal entirely circumvents free will. This is the God who willingly deceives "his" people, and then punishes them for the choices "he" moves them to make. Ellwood, in her collection *Batter My Heart*, calls this God the "nurturing betrayer" (or the "betraying nurturer.")[30] This is the God who promises to rain down plagues upon Egypt if Pharaoh does not repent, but then hardens Pharaoh's heart so that "he" may send the plagues in any case. This is the God who "was again roused to anger against

Israel; he incited David to harm them by saying, 'Go and number Israel and Judah'"[31] and then punished them for it. This is the God who blinds people to the truth, so that "his" wrath can come upon them when they do not "choose" rightly.

Most traditions have tried to integrate this aspect into their perspective, but it always seems to leave a bad taste in the mouth. It is reported in the Talmud that Rabbi Meiri said, "The Lord created the evil impulse, but He created Torah and repentance as its remedy. And the world is judged in mercy in that the sinner's repentance is found acceptable; and this is a merciful act of the Lord towards his creatures."[32] Yet from the earliest Hebrew prophets to the elaborate rationalizations of John Calvin, it is clear that the God of Betrayal is no one's friend.

In the eighth chapter of the book of Judges, we read that "during the time that Abimelech was prince over Israel, God sent an evil spirit to make mischief between Abimelech and the citizens of Shechem because the latter had played false to Abimelech."[33] It is God "himself" who contrived to stir up trouble for the king. The appearance of "an evil spirit from God" is a frequent occurrence in the Hebrew scriptures. In the first book of Samuel, we are told that the Holy Spirit of God had departed from King Saul, and that an "evil spirit" from God was terrorizing him. As a remedy, David was found to play soothing music, which seemed to help King Saul when he was under attack.

In the first book of Kings (chapter 22) the prophet Micaiah had a vision of God sitting on "his" throne, with all the heavenly hosts to the right and left. As Morrish tells the story,

Yahweh wants to know who would be willing to delude, entice or deceive King Ahab into marching to his death at Ramoth-gilead in a battle against the Syrians. After some preliminary discussion among the spirits, one of them comes forward and, standing before Yahweh, offers his services in this deception. "How will you do this?" asks Yahweh, as if intrigued by the possibilities of strategy and tactics in this operation. And the spirit answers, "By passing as a lying spirit into the mouth of all his prophets." ..."You shall delude them," replies Yahweh, "and you shall succeed also; pass out and do it." And so...Yahweh put a lying spirit into the mouths of all Ahab's prophets, and Yahweh "resolved on evil" for Ahab who subsequently died in a bloody battle.[34]

Yahweh tells the prophet Ezekiel in the sixth century B.C.E. that "when a prophet is beguiled into some prophetic utterance, it is I, Yahweh, who have beguiled him; I will strike at that prophet and I will destroy him out of my people Israel. They shall both suffer punishment."[35]

What is the reason for these ideas about God? We must remember that the idea of a devil, or Satan, would not be invented for many centuries yet. (We will deal with Satan at length later in this book.) But at this stage, as Morrish says, "no one among the Israelites could really envisage a power of evil set over against Yahweh: deception, beguilement, punishment, evil—all were as much the activity of Yahweh as were reward, sanctuary, compassion, and good."[36]

In fact, according to second Isaiah, Yahweh is recorded as saying,

I am Yahweh; there is no one else,
There is no God besides me:
Kings I disarm, but you I arm,
That east and west, men may confess
That I, Yahweh, stand alone—
There is no God besides me.
I form light and I make darkness,
I make peace and I create evil;
I, the Lord, the true God, do it all (Isaiah 45:7).

For the Jews, the greatest mystery is how God could let such horror befall them even though they have remained faithful. From ancient times through the 20th century conundrum of the Holocaust, the dilemma of Job is repeated again and again. The Psalmist expresses appropriate rage at this sort of betrayal.

In Psalm 44, we read,

> In God we have boasted continually,
> and we will give thanks to your name forever.
> Yet you have rejected us and abased us,
> and have not gone out with our armies.
> You made us turn back from the foe,
> and our enemies have gotten spoil.
> You have made us like sheep for slaughter,
> and have scattered us among the nations.
> You have sold your people for a trifle,
> demanding no high price for them.
> You have made us the taunt of our neighbors,
> the derision and scorn of those around us.
> You have made us a byword among the nations,
> a laughingstock among the peoples.
> All day long my disgrace is before me,
> and shame has covered my face
> at the words of the taunters and revilers,
> at the sight of the enemy and the avenger.
> All this has come upon us,
> yet we have not forgotten you,
> or been false to your covenant.
> Our heart has not turned back,
> nor have our steps departed from your way,
> yet you have broken us in the haunt of jackals,
> and covered us with deep darkness.
> If we had forgotten the name of our God,
> or spread out our hands to a strange god,

would not God discover this?

For he knows the secrets of the heart.

Because of you we are being killed all day long,

and accounted as sheep for the slaughter.

Rouse yourself! Why do you sleep, O Lord?

Awake, do not cast us off forever!

Why do you hide your face?

Why do you forget our affliction and oppression?

For we sink down to the dust;

our bodies cling to the ground.

Rise up, come to our help.

Redeem us for the sake of your steadfast love.[37]

This notion of evil finding its origin in God is not nearly as prevalent in the Christian scriptures, but neither is it entirely absent. In the Lord's Prayer, the Father is beseeched not to "lead us into temptation," but rather to "deliver us from evil." Thus, even for Jesus, the notion that it may be God "himself" that is responsible for our being led astray is not a foreign one.

Nor is this attitude absent in Paul's writings. In his second letter to the Thessalonians, Paul writes "and for this cause God shall send them strong delusion, that they should believe a lie, that they all might be damned who believed not the truth, but had pleasure in unrighteousness" (2:11-12). The unrighteousness of this sort of "divine entrapment" is precisely the sort of unsettling fact that festers unresolved in the back of many a pious believer's brain, providing the same sort of torment—conscious or unconscious—that such "evil spirits from God" have always done.

The God of Betrayal is in evidence in Islam as well. The Koran proclaims that "Allah leaves in error whom He will and guides whom He pleases,"[38] and informs us that "no misfortune befalls except by Allah's will." This Islamic form of predestination is important to the Muslim—as the Calvinistic understanding is to some Christians—in affirming God's absolute sovereignty over all of creation, which must include the minds of human beings, who are mere creatures and cannot exist outside the reach of Allah's control or omnipotence.

God's deceptive tendencies are not limited to the earth-bound human in Islam, it is interesting to note. The Koran says that even in Hell, Allah will "send down to the unbelievers devils who incite them to evil" (19:85). Note that in this passage the source of the evil is Allah, just as in the "evil spirit from the Lord" in the Hebrew tradition. In the Islamic mythos, Satan—who is called Iblis—is not "the enemy" because of open rebellion, but because he remained faithful to Allah, and was deceived by the Almighty into his "fallen" state (more on this in Chapter Seven).

Throughout my growing up, I heard repeatedly from the preachers who populated the pulpit of my church that Satan was "the great deceiver," but the history of religions is clear that the greater deceiver is God. From the trickster of polytheistic myth, to the incarnation of Vishnu as the teacher of heresy, to the God of Abraham who leads "his" people astray in order to "justify" punishing them, none are quite as dangerous as the gods who, humans have every right to expect, should be the most trustworthy of beings. As the myths and scriptures of nearly every tradition reveal, however, this trust is misplaced. I was right to cower in the dark as a teenager, and right to feel betrayed—but I did not yet even begin to grasp the magnitude of the Divine deception.

...I, except you enthrall me, never shall be free,
Nor ever chaste, except you ravish me.

John Donne

Chapter Four

The Gods of Rape

W hen I was a teenager, my family and I attended a fundamentalist Baptist church in the suburbs of Chicago. Our pastor, Brother "George," was a portly Texan who excelled at the hellfire and damnation style of preaching that Baptists love. One sermon that stands out, however, was aimed not at the lost souls in our midst, but at wives. "Women, submit to your husbands!" Brother George bellowed. "Men have needs that can only be fulfilled in the bedroom, and it is your Christian duty before God to make sure your husband is satisfied. 'I have a headache,' won't cut it, ladies. Refusing to submit to your husband in the bedroom is a sin before God!"

I had never seen a more mixed response to one of Brother George's sermons, and I was mesmerized by it. The men all shouted, "Amen!" in agreement, while one by one the women crossed their arms and glared at the pulpit, refusing to even make eye contact with Brother George. The only one looking straight at him was his own wife, and if looks could kill, Brother George would have been dead, buried, and forgotten by the end of his sermon.

Our family typically discussed the service in general—and the sermon, in particular—on the way home, but that night silence reigned in our car. The only conversation was a short one. "Sounds like Brother George isn't getting any," my mother said flatly.

"Nope," agreed my father, who turned up his beloved Country and Western music for the rest of the ride home. Even at such a young age, I was horrified by what I had witnessed. Brother George that night had attempted to coerce the women in our community into sexual activity against their will. Instead of a gun or knife, he had held the threat of God's judgment over their heads. I felt shame for him, although I was not completely clear why at the time. Now I know that Brother George was inciting rape in a sacred context, and am painfully aware that it was not an anomalous incident. The gods of rape are repeat offenders, and their sexual predation has been going on for a very long time indeed.

The Gods of Rape
in Polytheistic Religions

We may speak today of the environmental crisis as "the rape of the earth," but the archetypal precursor to this is the African Dogon myth of Amma, the Creator god. It seems he took clay and shaped the world in the form of a woman, who lay stretched out from North to South. Her pubic mound was an anthill, her clitoris a termite nest. This Amma immediately circumcised. Then Amma had sex with her.[1] The rape of the earth, indeed.

The Egyptians had a number of gods with dubious sexual habits. Among them is Sekhmet, the lioness-goddess who would often meet an unsuspecting man in the wilderness and seduce him. Once he was vulnerable, she would revert to her leonine form, tear him to shreds, and eat him. So voracious was her appetite that her child, the sun god, begged her to leave off so that some men might survive upon the earth.[2] Even though the sun god entreated his mother for mercy, he himself was no model of ethical behavior, since he frequently kidnapped any woman that caught his eye and had his way with her, including the goddesses Nuit and Isis.[3]

The presently popular Native American god Kokopelli, whose

whimsical form graces everything from drinking glasses to t-shirts, was known in his mythologies as one who seduces young girls, and brings babies (which, it seems, would follow naturally).[4] This sort of behavior was also rampant amongst the Greek pantheon, of course. Pan, horny in more ways than one, certainly seduced his share of maids and nymphs, but not all of them were as willing as he might hope. In one myth, he was obsessed with a water spirit named Syrinx. The water spirit, however, was a follower of Artemis, who advocated chastity. She rebuffed Pan's advances, but the goat god would not take no for an answer. He eventually trapped her, and in desperation, she cried out to her sisters to transform her into something, anything, that he would not violate. As soon as he pounced upon her she changed into a clump of reeds.[5]

Pan's career is filled with such encounters, but the most famous is with Selene. As Kerényi tells it, "the moon-goddess refused to company with the dark god. Whereupon Pan, to please her, dressed himself in white sheep-skins, and thus seduced Selene. He even carried her on his back."[6]

The greatest offender of the Greek pantheon is, however, undoubtedly Zeus himself. When his mother, Rhea, forbade him to marry, he went into a rage and tried to rape Rhea herself. "Rhea turned herself into a serpent. Zeus did likewise, and as serpent with serpent, entwined in an indissoluble knot, he coupled with her."[7] The result of this union was Zeus' daughter Persephone, whom he also ravished — also in the form of a serpent.[8] And the result of this further union was the god Dionysos, who was no mean offender on this score himself.[9]

In a similar story, Zeus found himself attracted to Nemesis. But when he approached her, the goddess ran away. She was overwhelmed by rage, which only grew as Zeus continued his pursuit of her. She jumped into the sea and assumed the form of a fish, but that did not slow Zeus down for a second — he plunged right into the sea after her. She again tried to escape him on land, assuming the form of a goose. But Zeus turned himself into a swan, who finally caught up with her and raped her.[10]

Zeus even raped his own sister, Hera, descending again as a swan during a storm to rest in her lap. When she took pity on the bird and covered him with her robe, Zeus assumed his own shape, and struggled with her until he promised to make her his wife, at which point she acquiesced, and the great god had his way.

Hera had her revenge however, for when it appeared that the Greeks might be overtaken by the Trojans, she contrived to distract Zeus by seducing him by means of a magic girdle.

Zeus also had a brutish way with matchmaking. When Aphrodite refused Zeus' advances, he forced her to marry the deformed god Hephaestus. And when Hades was attracted to Persephone, by means of Eros' nefarious arrows, Hades asked Zeus' permission to marry her. According to Rosenberg, Zeus replied,

> "Of course, I would be delighted to give you Persephone, dear brother," Zeus replied, "but our sister, Demeter, would never agree to such a marriage. She would not permit me to exchange Persephone's freedom to roam through her flower-filled fields, shimmering under the light from Lord Helios' chariot, for the opportunity to be queen in your dark kingdom.... However," the lord of Olympus concluded, "since you are my brother and the ruler of a mighty kingdom, if you insist on having Persephone, that would be a great honor for her. Although I cannot force my daughter to marry you, I shall secretly help you to seize her."

So it came about that one day, as Persephone was gathering flowers on one of the Sicilian meadows, she noticed in the distance an incredibly beautiful bloom that she had never seen before. Leaving her companions far behind, Persephone immediately ran over the fields toward this unusual flower. She had no way of knowing that her father secretly had commanded the earth to create this special flower as a lure in order to please Hades.

As Persephone reached toward the fragrant flower to add it to her collection, the earth suddenly opened wide, and out came a golden chariot drawn by black horses and driven by the dark lord himself. Keeping his left hand on the reigns, Hades extended his right arm, lifted Persephone off the ground, placed her beside him in the chariot, and drove off at top speed before Persephone's companions realized that she had disappeared.[11]

Persephone was confined to the dark god's lair, until Demeter withdrew her powers from the earth, leaving it bare and lifeless. Zeus then negotiated for Persephone's partial return.

The Gods of Rape in Hinduism

The Hindu deities are no strangers to sexual coercion, either, as we shall see. In one myth, from the Brhadaranyaka Upanishad, the world begins with a rape. The primal man, Purusha, looked around and found himself alone in the void, and he was afraid. But he took courage, and desired a partner, so he caused himself to fall into two parts, and Husband and Wife were born. He united with her, and she grew very upset at this incest, thinking, "How can he unite with me after engendering me from himself? For shame! I will conceal myself."

In a scene that is probably related to Zeus' pursuit of Nemisis, the Wife became a cow, after which the Husband became a bull. He united with her and thus began a population of cattle upon the earth. The Wife then turned herself into a mare. He, of course, became a stallion, and the first horses were born of their mating. Still trying to escape him, she transformed into a female ass, and he a male ass, and so on, until all the beasts of the field and fowls of the air were propagated.

What is horrifying about this passage is not simply that it is a rape (although one could make a case for Onanism here, since both halves were part of Purusha's body originally, but one could say the same for a mother and son, too, which would most assuredly be incest), but that it is serial rape: through all of the new woman's protestations, Purusha is unrepentant, dismissive of her entreaties, and pursues his own ends heedless of the pain or suffering caused to her. According to this myth, every animal that ever was owes its origination to violence.[12]

One of the greatest offenders was the king of the Vedic gods, Indra, who made the seduction and forcible rape of others' wives—especially the wives of holy men!—a sort of hobby. According to Daniélou, "Indra...took the disguise of King Rudmangada to seduce Mukunda, the wife of the sage Vacaknavi, who felt attracted toward the king (Genesa Purana 1.36.40). He seduced the wife of the sage Utathya and had to suffer grave consequences for this (Skanda Purana 2.7.23). He also seduced Ahalya, the wife of the sage Gautama. She was rejected by her husband and made invisible, while the sage's curse impressed upon Indra a thousand marks resembling the female organ as signs of his lewdness. Later these were ennobled into eyes...."[13]

In the Ramayana, Indra perpetrates an act that is at once rape, fratricide, abortion, and incest. It involves Indra's step-mother and aunt, Diti, whose sons the demons he has just slain. Diti was in deep mourning, and cried out to Kashyap Muni, her husband, "Lord, your strong sons have killed my own. I want to have a son who will kill Indra—I believe my asceticism can earn such a boon. Please grant me a child capable of killing Indra."

Kashyap Muni replied, "All right. You are a good woman, and your asceticism is indeed great. If you practice austerities and remain pure for a thousand years, you will have a son who will kill Indra on the battlefield." When he said this, Diti was glad. She went immediately to a temple and began her practice of austerities. Indra was impressed by her devotion, and supplied her with whatever she needed.

After 990 years, she promised Indra that she would soon have a child that would stand beside him in battle. After making this promise, she lay down for a nap. But she carelessly lay down with her head where her feet should be, which made her impure. Indra knew she was up to something, and when he saw how she had defiled herself, he laughed out loud. In his glee, Indra entered her womb, and cut the embryo into seven pieces. The embryo cried out in pain and alarm, and woke Diti. Indra cried, "Shut up!" to the embryo, and continued to slash it to bits. Diti realized with alarm what was happening inside her and shouted, "No! Do not destroy it!" Indra then had pity on his step-mother, and came out of her, still holding his weapon, the thunderbolt. Indra folded his palms together and bowed to her, saying respectfully, "I took advantage of your mistake, and have slain the one who would slay me. I beg your forgiveness."[14]

Whether Diti was able to forgive or not, the pieces of the embryo became the Maruts, Indra's wild confederates in battle. From a purely monarchical perspective, Indra was perfectly within his rights to preserve his throne, yet his means — penetrating a woman without her consent or knowledge, and performing a coerced abortion — cannot help but appall us.

In later mythology, Shiva inherited some of Indra's sexual trickery and prowess. In an Orissan creation myth, Shiva commanded Bhimsen to make houses for the primordial couple, who were brother and sister. This Bhimsen did, but because they lived in separate houses, they never copulated and did not have children. Bhimsen was not happy about this and told Shiva so. So Shiva took on the appearance of snakes, scorpions, and ants and scared the woman so badly she fled to her brother's bed for protection. This seemed like a good time to invent tickling, so Shiva did, and as the primal couple tickled each other, lust overcame them, and the human race began.[15]

In the Mahabharata, Shiva seems to have assumed Indra's fascination for the wives of holy men. He had become unsatisfied with his wife, and went naked into the Pine Forest, acting mad. His erect phallus went before him, and his thoughts were consumed with lust for the sages' wives.[16] Shiva was successful in his venture, and even confessed it, when confronted by the sages later in the myth.

In one myth from the Bhavisya Purana this lust for holy men's wives is shared by all three of Hinduism's chief gods. It seems that the lord Atri and his wife Anasuya were practicing their spiritual disciplines near the river Ganges. Atri was deeply meditating upon Brahman, when Brahma, Shiva, and Vishnu each approached him and told him to name a boon for himself. Atri heard their words, but was so focused on the ineffable Self that he would not be distracted to reply. So the gods went to speak to his wife Anasuya instead. When they saw her, Shiva's lingam sprang up and he stroked it as he gazed upon her. Vishnu was overwhelmed by his lust for her, and Brahma was so overcome that his godhood was temporarily suspended and he started accruing karma. Brahma said, "Have sex with me, or I will surely die, for you have made me drunk with desire."

Anasuya was true to her marriage vow, and so she refused them a response, for she was terrified of angering them. But the gods were not to be dissuaded, and they grabbed her and began to rape her. But Anasuya became so enraged that she cursed them, saying, "You will each be born as my sons, for you have been intoxicated by passion. The penis of Shiva, the head of Brahma, and the feet of Vishnu will forever more be worshipped by people, and the supreme gods will become a supreme joke, and everyone will laugh at you."

When they heard this curse, they came to their senses and released her. They bowed low before her and recited the Vedas to her. Then Anasuya softened and said, "When you have served your incarnations as my children, you will be released from my curse, and you will be content." So Brahma was born as Candramans, Shiva was born as Dattatraya, and Vishnu was born as Durvasas. Each of them became holy men in order to eradicate the evil they had done.[17]

The God of Rape
in the Abrahamic Religions

There is no place in the Jewish scriptural or apocryphal tradition where God "himself" rapes someone, but there are instances where "he" approves of rape and sexual abuse.[18]

When Israel attacked the Midianites, they killed everyone except for the women, children, and animals (Num. 31:7-18).[19] Moses was furious, and asked the generals, "Why have you let all the women live? These are the very ones who followed Balaam's advice and caused the people of Israel to rebel against the Lord at Mount Peor. They are the ones who caused the plague to strike the Lord's people. Now kill all the boys and all the women who have slept with a man. Only the young girls who are virgins may live; you may keep them for yourselves."

No one asked the young girls if they wanted to be kept, raped, and forced into domestic servitude. And unfortunately, this is not an isolated incident. When Moses was laying down God's rules for war, he told them, "When you draw near to a town to fight against it, offer it terms of peace. If it accepts your terms of peace and surrenders to you, then all the people in it shall serve you at forced labor. If it does not submit to you peacefully, but makes war against you, then you shall besiege it; and when the Lord your God gives it into your hand, you shall put all its males to the sword. You may, however, take as your booty the women, the children, livestock, and everything else in the town, all its spoil. You may enjoy the spoil of your enemies, which the Lord your God has given you" (Deut. 20:10-14). Apparently, for the God of Israel, rape is simply business as usual.

In another account, when the people of Israel were engaged in the "ethnic cleansing" of Canaan, twelve thousand Israelite soldiers were sent to Jabesh-Giliad and ordered to kill everyone, including children and all women who were not virgins (Jud. 21:10-24). After the battle, they counted four hundred virgins, and brought them back to their camp. They decided to give them to the men of the tribe of Benjamin, who were powerfully short on women at the time. Nobody asked the women whether they thought this was a good idea, but the biblical author is not concerned with their opinions.

But the four hundred virgins were apparently not enough. So the leaders of Israel told the men of Benjamin to go to the religious feast at Shiloh, and to hide out in the vineyards, saying, "Go and lie in wait in the vineyards, and watch; when the young women of Shiloh come out to dance in the dances, then come out of the vineyards and each of you carry off a wife for himself from the young women of Shiloh, and go to the land of Benjamin. Then if their fathers or their brothers come to complain to us, we will say to them, 'Be generous and allow us to have them; because we did not capture in battle a wife for each man. But neither did you incur guilt by giving your daughters to them.'"

In instances where men are raping without divine sanction, God certainly does not think it a very serious offense. The Mosaic Law commands, "If a man happens to meet a virgin who is not pledged to be married and rapes her and they are discovered, he shall pay the girl's father fifty shekels of silver. He must marry the girl, for he has violated her. He can never divorce her as long as he lives" (Deut. 22:28, NIV). Not only is this "punishment" a slap on the wrist for the rapist, it condemns the innocent woman to a lifetime of unwanted sexual congress with her rapist. It is hard to imagine a more chilling scenario, especially one disguising as "justice." Only if the woman is already married can the rapist be put to death (Deut. 22:25).

But wait, it gets worse. In an argument in the Talmud over Leviticus 15, regarding whom and what is rendered ritually unclean if a menstruating woman is raped, Rabbi Rabina declared, "Therefore a gentile girl who is three years and one day old, since she is then suitable to have sexual relations, also imparts uncleanness of the flux variety. That is self-evident!"[20]

Self evident, indeed! One would like to think that the notion that a three-year-old girl is suitable for sexual intercourse is a mistake, but it is not. According to this tradition, then, for the mere price of fifty shekels, any three-year-old girl was fair game to pederasts, who can then marry the child, and may enjoy her at his leisure with impunity — so long as she was not Jewish and had not already been promised in marriage to someone.

Nor is the God of Israel a stranger to sexual abuse. In Jeremiah 13:25-26, we read "This is your fate, the portion measured out to you by me, says the Lord, because you have forgotten me and put your trust in that which is false. I shall surely cover your face with your skirts and your personal parts will be seen." Isaiah 3:16-17 likewise warns, "The Lord said: Since the daughters of Zion have grown haughty, walking with stretched-forth necks and roving eyes, provocative in their steps and wiggling their feet, the Lord will smite the head of the daughters of Zion with scabs and will expose their personal parts." Public stripping and humiliation, are, it seems, fit punishments for normal teenage vanity in God's purview.

A further account of sexual abuse is recorded in the book of the prophet Ezekiel:

I passed by you, and saw you flailing about in your blood. As you lay in your blood, I said to you, "Live! and grow up like a plant of the field." You grew up and became tall and arrived at full womanhood; your breasts were formed, and your hair had grown; yet you were naked and bare. I passed by you again and looked on you; you were at the age for love. I spread the edge of my cloak over you, and covered your nakedness: I pledged myself to you and entered into a covenant with you, says the Lord GOD, and you became mine....

Thus says the Lord God, Because your lust was poured out

and your nakedness uncovered in your whoring with your lovers, and because of all your abominable idols, and because of the blood of your children that you gave to them, therefore, I will gather all your lovers, with whom you took pleasure, all those you loved and all those you hated; I will gather them against you from all around, and will uncover your nakedness to them, so that they may see all your nakedness.

I will judge you as women who commit adultery and shed blood are judged, and bring blood upon you in wrath and jealousy. I will deliver you into their hands, and they shall throw down your platform and break down your lofty places; they shall strip you of your clothes and take your beautiful objects and leave you naked and bare. They shall bring up a mob against you, and they shall stone you and cut you to pieces with their swords. They shall burn your houses and execute judgments on you in the sight of many women; I will stop you from playing the whore, and you shall also make no more payments. So I will satisfy my fury on you, and my jealousy shall turn away from you; I will be calm, and will be angry no longer.[21]

Jewish scholar David Blumenthal points out that after "his" subjects' humiliation, reconciliation is then possible for God. "God is the abusive husband," says Blumenthal, "who goes through the well-known fight-beat-reconcile cycle. God wounds, heals, and wounds again."[22] We may at least take comfort in the fact that this is only a figurative humiliation, since the woman in Ezekiel's passage is not an actual woman, but symbolic of Israel herself.

It is only in Gnostic Christianity that we see evidence of the Hebrew God actually raping someone physically. In the Secret Book of John, discovered in 1945 as part of the cache of Gnostic scripture at Nag Hammadi, Egypt, we discover the following, "When Yaldabaoth [Yaweh] realized that the humans had withdrawn from him, he cursed his earth. He found the woman as she was preparing herself for her husband. He was master over her. And he did not know the mystery that had come into being through the sacred plan. The two of them were afraid to denounce [Yaweh]. He displayed to his angels the ignorance within him. He threw the humans out of paradise and cloaked them in thick darkness."[23]

In a similar document, the Reality of the Rulers, it is not God himself who rapes Eve, but his angels, or "authorities":

Then the authorities came up to their Adam. And when they saw his female counterpart speaking with him, they became agitated with great agitation; and they became enamored of her. They said to one another, "Come, let us sow our seed in her," and they pursued her. And she laughed at them for their folly and their blindness; and in their clutches she became a tree, and left before them a shadow of herself resembling herself; and they defiled it foully. And they defiled the seal of her voice, so that by their modeled form, together with their own image, they made themselves liable to condemnation.[24]

Harold Bloom has pointed out numerous parallels between Gnosticism and Mormonism,[25] and indeed, a similar incident is reported in Brigham Young's Journal of Discourses. Only this time, it is not Eve that is raped, but the "virgin" Mary, who may or may not have given her consent. Young writes,

When our father Adam came into the garden of Eden, he came into it with a celestial body, and brought Eve, one of his wives, with him. He helped to make and organize this world. He is Michael, the Archangel, the Ancient of Days! — about whom holy men have written and spoken — He is our Father and our God, and; the only god with whom we have to do. Every man upon the earth, professing Christians or non-professing, must hear it, and will know it sooner or later.... When the Virgin Mary conceived the child Jesus, the Father had begotten him in his own likeness. He was not begotten by the Holy Ghost. And who is the Father? He is the first of the human family; and when he took a tabernacle, it was begotten by his Father in heaven, after the same manner as the tabernacles of Cain, Abel, and the rest of the sons and daughters of Adam and Eve.... Jesus, our elder brother, was begotten in the flesh by the same character that was in the garden of Eden, and who is our Father in Heaven.[26]

Whether or not the child Mary consented, the act of a several-hundred-thousand-year-old being having sex with a twelve-year-old girl is likely to be considered statutory rape in our time. (Though to be fair, we should note that the minimum age for marriage in Brigham's time averaged ten years, and many of those were "arranged," a nice euphemism for marriage without the girls' consent.)

Then there is the power differential to take into consideration. Would Mary have felt safe saying "No" to the Creator? Probably not, and it was therefore sexual abuse and an abuse of power for God/Adam/Michael/The Ancient of Days to have even approached her in the first place.

Although we must go pretty far afield from orthodox Christianity to find instances of rape by God, the orthodox support of human rape is clearly found in the Epistles of Paul. The verse used by Brother George in the opening story of this chapter was not twisted by him in order to force his wife's conjugal cooperation. Paul's admonition, "wives, submit to your husbands" (Eph 5:22-24) has long been used to enforce the male will in the bedroom.

In Islam, we find a whole host of new horrors. Shariah, Islamic Law, does not honor the testimony of women in sexual cases. If a woman says she is raped, and if there is no physical evidence to support her story, she must produce four male witnesses to the act, and the rapist must himself confess—otherwise she will be condemned to die for adultery.[27] For this reason, women are frequently raped in Islamic society as a form of revenge against the women's fathers, brothers, or husbands. Their noses are frequently cut off during the attack to forever mark them as "damaged goods," and the women are often either abandoned to mental institutions or encouraged to kill themselves to spare their families shame.

While this seems to us most unfair to Islamic women, the fate of non-Muslim women under Muslim control is far worse. When a Muslim army captured the army of Banu l-Mustaliq at the well of Muraysi in 626 CE, Mohammad took Juwayriyya, the chieftain's daughter, as his sixth wife. He also told his men that they could have intercourse with any of the women they chose so long as they pulled out before ejaculating.[28] This is far from an isolated incident. While going out against "infidels," Mohammad elsewhere also promised his warriors, "Allah will soon make you inherit their land, their treasures, and make you sleep with their women."[29]

One ancient chronicler, Abu Sa'id al-Khudri, wrote:

The Apostle of Allah sent a military expedition to Awtas on the occasion of the battle of Hunain. They met their enemy and fought with them. They defeated them and took them captives. Some of the Companions of the Apostle of Allah were reluctant to have intercourse with the female captives in the presence of their husbands who were unbelievers. So Allah, the Exalted, sent down the Koranic verse: "And all married women (are forbidden) unto you save those (captives) whom your right hand possess" [Koran 4:24].[30]

Allah seems all too eager to provide new revelations to justify the Muslims' rape of women who were completely helpless according to the norms of their culture. Not only are captives fair game, but slaves are, too. According to the Bukhari Hadith, the King of Egypt sent Mohammad a gift of two Christian slave girls. The prophet kept one of them as a concubine, and enjoyed her so much that he visited her many times in a given day. When his wives became jealous and demanded that he stop seeing her, Mohammad complied.

But then Allah conveniently provided a new section of the Koran that chastised the prophet for allowing himself to be browbeaten by his wives, and warned the jealous women "perhaps if he divorces you, God will give him in exchange better wives than you...penitent, obedient...both known of men and virgins. O believers, save yourselves...from the fire whose fuel is men and stones" (Koran 66:5-6). No mention is made as to how the Christian slave girl felt about the situation—apparently, it is a non-issue.

While this seems to us barbaric in our day and age, contemporary Muslim holy men have made pronouncements that surpass even Mohammad's in their outrageous cruelty. In 1990, the Ayatollah Khomeini wrote:

A man can have sexual pleasure from a child as young as a baby. However he should not penetrate, sodomizing the child is okay. If the man penetrates and damages the child then he should be responsible for her subsistence all her life. This girl, however, does not count as one of his four permanent wives. The man will not be eligible to marry the girl's sister.... It is better for a girl to marry in such a time when she would begin menstruation at her husband's house rather than her father's home. Any father marrying his daughter so young will have a permanent place in heaven.[30]

Far from being consigned to the myths of the past, the God of Rape is horrifyingly alive and well. Even if it is not God "himself" doing the raping, this God is all too eager to empower others to do it for "him," perpetuating yet another aspect of this monstrous deity.

"I am time, inclined
toward destroying the worlds."

Bhagavad Gita 11:52

Chapter Five

The Gods of Genocide

One of my earliest memories of Sunday School is marching alongside the other children in mock formation, pretending I was holding a rifle, singing gleefully, "I may never march in the infantry, ride in the cavalry, shoot the artillery. I may never zoom! o'er the enemy, but I'm in the Lord's army!..."

I had no idea what I was saying. A few years later, I was traumatized by the images of the Vietnam war on television, and couldn't sleep. I was beginning to get it. Religion has always had a strong militaristic streak. Even our liturgies are shot through with militaristic language glorifying warfare and God's participation in it. "Holy, holy holy," we sing in the Sanctus, "Lord God of hosts..." The Lord of armies, the God of war. I remember Brother George, the pastor of the arch-fundamentalist church we attended while I was in high school, lamenting the economic recession, and preaching that what this country needed was a war to pull it up by its bootstraps! I shifted uncomfortably in my seat and looked around. I could see I was not the only one uncomfortable with this statement. The fact that he was more concerned with the economy than the lives of the young men who would die—or even the lives of those they would be sent to kill—was chilling to me, even then.

It seems that to the gods—and those that herald them—life is cheap. The records of our religious traditions certainly seem to support this statement, as they are filled with more bloodshed than every season of TV violence put together. Even more horrifying, it is not random violence, a person here, a person there. It is violence on a vast scale: entire populations have been murdered, men, women, children, and sometimes animals, all in the name of religion. The deities that call for such slaughter are the gods of genocide, and they are legion.

The Gods of Genocide
in Native Traditions

The ancient Mayan deities are a good example. In the Popol Vuh, the story of the creation is told. Before anything came to be, the creators were floating in the water, covered with colored feathers. They commanded the earth to emerge, and it did. They called forth the trees, and they came. They spoke of the animals, and the creatures emerged. The gods thought this would satisfy them, but the animals could not talk, and were only interested in food. The creators wanted someone who would talk to them, praise them, and love them.

So they created a man, and fashioned him out of mud. But the creature they made was too soft—he was weak, and his mind was weak, too. So they destroyed the man they had made.

Next, they decided to fashion humans out of wood. These were more successful, and numerous, but they had no soul, and did not give due consideration to the gods. So the gods determined to destroy them, too. They rained great chunks of sap from the sky to kill them, and moved the wild creatures to tear them limb from limb. Fires leaped up to burn them, and the caves refused them shelter. Very few of them survived—but some did, and we know them as monkeys today.

Finally, the gods formed men out of cornmeal and husks, but these were too wise, and threatened to know more than the gods themselves! So the gods blew fog into their faces so that they could not see properly. The gods then fashioned wives for them, and they praised their creators and reproduced widely. They also begged for light, and the creators were moved to create the sun to please them. The people were happy with this gift, and they danced and sang praises to the gods, and loved them.[1]

The treatment of their many "children" by the Mayan gods seems cruel and heartless, but it is far from unusual. The Mayans' neighbors, the Aztecs were little better. Their creator, Lord Con Ticci Viracocha created a race of giants who lived in darkness (for this was before the creation of the sun). But the giants' behavior displeased him, so he turned them all to stone, and then sent a flood to kill all the animals.[2]

The Aztecs' religious ceremonies echoed the violence of their creator, for their rituals demanded the sacrifice of 20,000 victims per year. The priests told them that without these sacrifices, the sun would not rise. So throughout the year, Aztec warriors would gather prisoners of war from surrounding tribes for the annual sacrifice. It would take the priests four straight days, working in eight teams to slaughter all 20,000 prisoners in due ritual fashion. Flesh from the prisoners' arms was consumed as part of this ritual, and their skulls were preserved on enormous racks, each of which held more than 10,000 heads.[3]

Aztecs were not only cruel to their neighbors, their own kind received some rough treatment as well. As James Haught writes, "Weeping children were sacrificed so that their tears might induce the rain god to water the crops. To please the maize goddess, dancing virgins were seized, decapitated, and skinned—and their skins were worn by priests in continued dancing."[4]

Wiping out early populations of humans seems to be a favorite sport amongst the monster gods, and floods were a popular means to this end. The Greeks tell the story of Zeus, who was disappointed with how wicked humankind had become. He visited the palace of King Lycaon, and announced himself. The king did not believe him, and tested the king of the gods by presenting him a platter of "fine meats" that turned out to be the boiled body parts of a man. Zeus, who despised human sacrifice, was so enraged that he killed everyone in the palace except for Lycaon, who turned into the animal most resembling his heart—a wolf—and scampered into the wilderness.

But Zeus' rage was not exhausted. He called forth all of his rain clouds, and enlisted the help of Poseidon. Together, they unleashed a torrent of rain and flood that threatened to drown every human being alive. Prometheus saw what was happening, and called to his son Deucalion in a dream, commanding him to build a boat large enough for himself, his wife, and supplies. For nine days and nights Deucalion and his wife floated safely. When Zeus saw that the only people left alive were this good and god-fearing couple, he laid aside his rage, and permitted them to live.[5]

The Hebrews, too, have a story of God wiping out all human life, with the exception of Noah, who was commanded to build an ark large enough for himself, his family, and two of every kind of beast to repopulate the earth once the waters had receded (Gen. 6-9).

The Gods of Genocide in Hinduism

We have already heard of how Vishnu tricked the demons of the Triple City into believing the false doctrine of the Buddha, but it was Shiva who actually destroyed the city and killed all that dwelt therein. This aspect of Shiva is also known as Hara, "the remover," that aspect which destroys all things. Daniélou says,

In the Mahabharata, Rudra is "he who sweeps away all beings." He is also the "remover of the eyes of Bhaga," since he blinded Bhaga, the Aditya who distributes to the gods their shares of the sacrifice. He is the "remover of the offerings of Ritual Skill," for he steals away the fruit of the sacrifice... Hara is disease and his messenger is fever. He is death, which destroys indiscriminately the good and the bad. At the end of the ages he devours all he has created. He draws in the universe and swallows up all things.[6]

Shiva is good at this sort of business—he is variously known as "the Great Fear," "the Wrathful," "the Fury," "the Fearful," "the Terrible," "the Frightful," "the Lord of Ghosts," and "Death, the Remover," among other horrific titles. While Shiva, as the Lord of Death, devours everyone in their season, he is the god of genocide par excellence, in that, at the end of the age, it is Shiva who will devour all things. "You are the origin of the worlds," says the Mahabharata, "and you are Time, their destroyer."[7]

The goddesses in Hindu myth are likewise bloody, and, as we have seen, often threaten to spin out of control in their bloody rampages. Usually summoned to dispatch a nasty demon whom none of the other gods can thwart, the bloodlust of the goddesses is inflamed in battle, and frequently threatens to destroy the world if not brought under control by the other gods. Both Durga and Kali are frequently employed, and both share an anger management problem that threatens all life, human and animal.

Vishnu, too, is not opposed to killing sprees. In the Bhagavad Gita, he counseled Arjuna on the eve of battle in the form of his incarnation, Krishna. Arjuna's spirit has failed him at the thought of going into battle against his cousins, his beloved teachers, and other friends and family. But Vishnu reveals to him that the lives of his loved ones, and indeed his life, too, are but illusions. In reality, says Krishna, there is only one being in the universe, and that is Krishna himself. "And I never die," he tells Arjuna. Krishna entreats Arjuna to go forth and kill his enemies with a glad heart, since none of them are real, and therefore cannot really die. He allows Arjuna a glimpse of his true form, and Arjuna sees all of creation as being a great, kaleidoscopic manifestation of the One Lord, Vishnu, and is convinced. He goes into battle, with Krishna serving as his charioteer, and crushes his beloved foe.

As late as the 19th century, devotees of Kali were sacrificing a staggering number of people, some estimate as high as 20,000 victims a year. The sect was known as the Thugees, which is the source of our slang word, "thug." Thugees would strangle travelers, believing that Brahma was producing souls faster than Shiva could destroy them. The Thugees were commanded by Kali to balance the scales through their "devotional" efforts.[8]

The God of Genocide
in Monotheistic Faiths

The God of Israel seems particularly fond of genocide. It is hard to count the number of times it is advocated in the Hebrew scriptures, there are so many—so a few examples must suffice. In Deuteronomy 2:31-34, Moses reports,

> The Lord came to me, "See, I have begun to give Sihon and his land over to you. Begin now to take possession of his land." So when Sihon came out against us, he and all his people for battle at Jahaz, the Lord our God gave him over to us; and we struck him down, along with his offspring and all his people. At that time we captured all his towns, and in each town we utterly destroyed men, women, and children. We left not a single survivor.

This is far from an anomalous event. Only three verses later, having just wiped out the people of Sihon, the Israelites are having at the Bashanites. Moses sums up this bloody episode, saying, "We utterly destroyed them, as we had done to King Sihon of Heshbon, in each city utterly destroying men, women, and children" (see Deut. 3:1-7).

Such genocidal tactics were not just a feature of Moses' leadership, but became the modus operandi of the Israelite nation. We all remember the Battle of Jericho, where Joshua, Moses' successor, has his army march around the city seven times and blow their trumpets. Everyone knows the miraculous result: "The people shouted, and the trumpets were blown. As soon as the people heard the sound of the trumpets, they raised a great shout, and the wall fell down flat; so the people charged straight ahead into the city and captured it." But few include the ghastly details that follow in the very next verse when recounting this tale: "Then they devoted to destruction by the edge of the sword all in the city, both men and women, young and old, oxen, sheep, and donkeys" (Joshua 6:20-21).

It is tempting to lay such shameful behavior at the feet of Israel's leadership instead of their God, but the biblical record is very clear on this score. The prophet Samuel said to King Saul, "Thus says the Lord of hosts, 'I will punish the Amalekites for what they did in opposing the Israelites when they came up out of Egypt. Now go and attack Amalek, and utterly destroy all that they have; do not spare them, but kill both man and woman, child and infant, ox and sheep, camel and donkey'" (1 Sam. 15:2-3).

Saul obeys this command to the letter—almost. He kills all of the people with the single exception of the king, whom he takes captive. Nor does he slaughter the livestock, but takes them for a later sacrifice to God. For this disobedience, God curses Saul, saying, "I regret that I made Saul king, for he has turned back from following me, and has not carried out my commands" (1 Sam. 15:11). After a lengthy and emotional confrontation, Samuel then tells Saul, "I will not return with you; for you have rejected the word of the Lord, and the Lord has rejected you from being king over Israel." As Samuel turned to go, Saul clutched at his robe, and tore it. Samuel turned back and pronounced, "The Lord has torn the kingdom of Israel from you this very day..." (1 Sam. 15:26-28).

For all of their talk of following "the prince of peace," Christians have been just as bad. The infamous witch-hunts of the middle ages attempted to root out covens of women who were in league with the Devil, and were "guilty" of oppressing innocent people—and even whole villages—through their sorcery. In reality, no such covens existed. Instead, the witch hunts provided a convenient excuse for communities to purge themselves of any woman who honored the religious traditions of her ancestors, attempted to heal through knowledge of herbs or other traditional means, got "out of line," or was in any way unusual or exceptional.

Some researchers estimate that in the five hundred years that witches were being hunted—either by the Catholic church, or later, by the even more rabid Protestant reformers—over nine million women lost their lives. While some complain that this estimate is high, there is no dispute that the witch-hunts constituted a holocaust of tremendous proportions that has thus far gone largely unacknowledged and unmourned.

No community has suffered such a prolonged and continuous assault by Christians as have the Jews, however. From the beginning of the Christian church, an insidious anti-Semitism has been cultivated. Beginning in the twelfth century, wave after wave of attacks upon Jewish communities in Europe began. One typical story was that of twelve-year-old William of Norwich. The boy was found dead, and a monk spread rumors that the Jewish community had sacrificed him and used his blood in a horrific group ritual. Another monk, Thomas of Monmouth, picked up that ball and ran with it, fabricating and publishing a fantastic and outrageously inflammatory tract that described alleged rituals common to the Jews that routinely involved the sacrifice of Christian children. These stories circulated quickly and widely, and reports of such Jewish "crimes" snowballed exponentially.[9]

In addition to sacrificing Christian children, Jews were also accused of stealing consecrated hosts and mutilating them, sometimes driving nails into them, in order to crucify Jesus again. As such stories proliferated, they were ornamented by such details as the hosts crying out in pain, bleeding, or turning into doves and flying away.[10]

The Christian retaliation for such absurd accusations is impossible to accurately compile, as it was so widespread and cruel. In 1285, 180 Jews were burned in Munich; in 1294 all of the Jews in Bern were executed; 628 Jews were killed in Nuremberg in 1298, including the famous scholar Mordecai ben Hillel; in 1337 the whole Jewish community was killed at Deggendorf, Bavaria; the same fate met the entire Jewish population of Tent, Italy in 1475. The Bavarian knight Rindfliesch led a team that exterminated 146 Jewish communities in a six-month period alone.[11]

The Russian pogroms of the nineteenth century were just as bloody—and pointless. These were politically-motivated slaughters, in which the medieval slanders of child-sacrifice were resurrected in a devious and calculated scapegoating campaign.

For all of the hostility leveled at the pagans and Jews, Christians have fared no better at the hands of their fellows. In the mid-twelfth century an offshoot of the Gnostics called the Cathars arose in southern France. The teachings were really not that appealing—it included a fierce celibacy, even for laypeople. But the Roman Catholic clergy had become so lazy and corrupt that the people were drawn to the Cathars largely due to their true piety and sincerity.

The Cathars were converting huge numbers, which, of course, was an intolerable situation for the Roman Catholic Church. Many nobles in that area were Cathars, and so in 1204, they began to fortify one of their strongholds, Montsegur, and readied it for battle. In 1209 an entire crusade was launched against them, the first crusade directed at fellow Christians (even if those Christians were "heretics").

A madman named Simon de Montfort led the charge, and whole villages of Cathars were brutally massacred. When asked how the crusaders would be able to tell the Cathars from the Catholics, the papal legate Arnaud sneered, "Kill them all. God will know his own."

The Cathars were determined, however, and their castle at

Montsegur withstood the crusaders' attacks. In 1215 the Inquisition was founded, and the crusaders renewed their charge. After six months of brave defense, Montsegur finally fell to the crusaders through an act of treachery, and in March 1244, the Cathars were captured.

Two hundred and five Cathars were led down the mountain, singing hymns with their heads held high. They marched straight into the bonfires built for them and perished. Whatever remnant of the Cathars that remained either went East to the Balkans, or they were absorbed into Catholic Christianity.[12]

All of this in the name of God, or at the behest of "authorities" allegedly taking their orders from God.

Allah has proved no more beneficent or merciful than Yahweh or Christ, unfortunately. The Koran is very clear about the treatment that unbelievers should receive:

> Let not those who disbelieve think that they can escape punishment. Truly, they will never be able to save themselves from Allah's punishment. Prepare all the force you can against them, including steeds of war to threaten the enemy of Allah and your enemy...O Prophet! Urge the believers to fight. If there are twenty steadfast persons amongst you, they will overcome two hundred, and if there be a hundred steadfast persons they will overcome a thousand of those who disbelieve, because the disbelievers are people who do not understand. It is not for a Prophet that he should have prisoners of war to be ransomed until he has slaughtered his enemies in the land. You desire the good of this world, but Allah desires for you the Hereafter (8:59-60, 65, 67).

Mohammad was hardest on the followers of native traditions, who were given the choice of conversion or death, while Jews and Christians were permitted to maintain their own faith, albeit with heavy taxes levied against them.

It was according to this doctrine of "convert or die" that Islam moved in waves over Palestine, Syria, Iraq, Persia, and Egypt in a hundred-year campaign of blood and religious fervor. Most chose conversion, obviously—at least an outward, nominal conversion. Some traditions, like Sufism, simply reclothed earlier, native religions in Islamic dress and were therefore tolerated.

Since Mohammad was perhaps closer to the source and received "divine" instruction as to when and how to apply Allah's commands, his successors have had to interpret Allah's will based on the examples in the Koran and the Hadith (the traditions of the Prophet). This leaves a lot of room for interpretation, and often those interpretations have been on the bloody side. How many of these campaigns of slaughter throughout the centuries were actually the will of Allah is a matter open for discussion, and it is a subject about which even devout Muslims are bound to disagree, especially since some of their bloodiest campaigns have not been against unbelievers, but against fellow Muslims who simply disagree.

This kind of bloodshed continues to the present day. In the 1880s, the "holy man" Mohammad Ahmad declared that he was divinely guided (Mahdi) and led a jihad against the Egyptian army, slaughtering 10,000 men. The British responded to this threat with force, and retaliated, and in a single day slaughtered 20,000 of Ahmad's followers.[13]

Muslims have also been particularly harsh on minority religions that arose or persisted in their midst. The Islamic Turkish government brutally massacred more than 600,000 Armenian Christians in their midst in 1915, tortured others, and drove even more into exile.[14] The Yizidis have also suffered terribly at the hands of their Muslim neighbors, and the Baha'is have been the target of wave after wave of torture, imprisonment, and murder. In the 1980s alone, over 300,000 Baha'is were persecuted in Iran, and about 200—including women and children— were executed. 40,000 Baha'is fled the Iranian persecution, scattering across the globe, and bringing the Baha'i message of interfaith cooperation and nonviolence to the world.

These "holy wars" are far from over, as the rhetoric of the "jihad" and "crusade" are to be found on the front page of American newspapers on any given day. The heinous terrorist attacks and the unprovoked and shameless slaughter in Iraq are horrifying evidence that the gods of genocide are alive and well.

That old Sunday School song still send shivers down my spine: "I may never march in the infantry, ride in the cavalry, shoot the artillery..." but plenty of others have, to the great and murderous destruction of millions upon millions of innocents, victims of those who fancied themselves soldiers in "the Lord's army."

God will then set up a bridge over Gehenna
and intercession will be allowed,
and they will say,
"O God, keep safe, keep safe."
The believers will then pass over
like the twinkling of an eye, like lightning,
like wind, like a bird,
like the finest horses and camels.
Some will escape and be kept safe,
some will be lacerated by flesh-hooks and thorns
which will rise up from Gehenna and let go,
and some will be pushed into the fire of Gehenna.

Hadith of Bukhari and Muslim

Chapter Six

The Gods of Judgment

T hough it rarely rears its head in mainline Protestant or Catholic churches, the cry of "Jesus is coming!" is pervasive in evangelical churches around the world. It can seem like a whole other world if you're not prepared for it. It is, however, the world I was raised in, and by the time I started high school the Second Coming of Christ and the Great Judgment it heralded dominated nearly every church service and sermon I heard.

When I was a freshman in high school, I invited some friends to come to our youth group meeting on Friday night. Usually our explicit activities, such as a movie or a party, were advertised, but there was a great cloud of secrecy about this particular event. We were simply encouraged to bring our friends and be ready for anything.

When my mother swung onto the long driveway of the church with a van full of youth group kids, we found our way impeded by a roadblock. Bright lights were shone in our eyes, and men in unfamiliar uniforms approached us. "Got any Bibles in this car, ma'am?" One of them asked my mother. "Any Bibles in there?!" another shouted at us. The doors were opened, and we were ordered out of the van, which they then searched. Our bibles were thrown into a basket as one of the guards took my mother aside. She then drove off, and we were escorted up to the church property.

All of the electricity seemed to be out, and the second story of the Fellowship Hall was lit only with candles. There were about 50 of us teenagers huddled in the cold and dark with no explanation, no idea what was to come next. After about a half hour, somebody started singing hymns—low, mournful songs about hope and deliverance. About fifteen minutes later, Brother George, Jr. came up the stairs. He was twenty-one years old, a superlative extemporaneous preacher, and our youth pastor.

Tonight he seemed to be broken beyond his years, however. He was shaking and pale. He couldn't look any of us in the eyes, and we were all instantly concerned. Falteringly, he took the podium and appeared to be choking back tears. When he finally did speak it was strained and sorrowful.

"This morning they came and took my Daddy away." He was speaking about our pastor, Brother George, Sr. "They charged him with preaching the Gospel of Jesus Christ, and right in front of my very eyes they handcuffed him and pistol-whipped him. The forced him to his knees and demanded that he renounce his Lord and Savior, Jesus Christ. 'No' he shouted, over and over. 'I will never renounce him.' Then my Daddy began to sing, 'Blessed Assurance, Jesus is Mine.' They hit my Daddy on the head, and he kept singing. Then one of them put a gun to his temple, and pulled the trigger. I watched my Daddy die today."

He took a moment to get a grip on himself. "And now they are coming after me. And if you are not willing to renounce Jesus Christ as your Lord and Savior, they will be coming after you. It is the beginning of the end, my friends. America has been conquered by a malevolent force. The Antichrist is rising, and the persecution of the church is beginning."

We met these words with both fear and hope, for we had been told such things would occur just before Jesus came back to rapture us away into heaven—and just before all of those nasty unbelievers would meet their doom. We sang a few more songs, and then we heard the door being battered down one story below us. As we continued to sing, the men in the unfamiliar uniforms burst into the room, waving their weapons and telling us all to stay seated and calm. Of course the girls were screaming, and we were all terrified. They grabbed Brother George and tied his hands behind his back. They forced him downstairs and out onto the moonlit lawn below. We watched out of the second story window as the uniformed men forced him to his knees and kicked him. We saw him shaking his head and screaming. Then we watched in silence as one of the men raised a pistol to his head and fired.

Brother George's head snapped forward, and he collapsed to the grass. Wordlessly we were escorted downstairs. Then the sirens began.

This kind of psychodrama was everyday fare in the church I was a part of during high school, and it was not unusual. They all served what we then believed to be a very important purpose: to prepare us for the great and terrible day of the Lord, when Jesus would return, Satan would hold sway over the earth, and the quick and the dead would alike be judged and sent to their eternal punishment or reward. We had to be strong, because the tribulation that preceded that time of trial would be severe, and every church service was filled with tasty bits of international gossip, each one another piece to add to our prophesy puzzle, to reassure us that the end was near and our faith was not in vain.

This kind of faith, I have come to see, is both sadistic and masochistic. Every hint of oppression against our variety of faith was met with glee, since it meant that Jesus was just around the corner; and we gloried in long and elaborately gory sermons about the fate of all those who did not share our peculiar theology. We loved to hear about how they would suffer, for it made us feel special and, most especially, *righteous*.

What we weren't told in any of those sermons was that the God that promoted such religious arrogance and cruelty was not ours alone—the gods of judgment go back a very long way indeed, and aspirants who gloried in the suffering of others nearly as far.

The Gods of Judgment
in Polytheistic Religions

In the Egyptian tradition, the god of judgment was Ma'at, who was the personification of justice and order. She was usually pictured as a woman with an enormous feather on her head, the symbol of truth. In the beginning, she was born of Ra, the sun god, when he emerged from the waters of Nun (chaos). It is Ma'at who held chaos at bay, and it was upon her that Egyptian society was ordered.

When an Egyptian died, they believed that the deceased heart was weighed against Ma'at (or her feather). If the heart was heavy with sin, then Ma'at's daughter Ammut, a fierce demonic character, devoured the soul, which was then dead forever. But if the heart and the feather were equal in weight, then the soul was ushered into Osirus' realm, the land of the dead.

Ma'at is just, but not that scary—that role falls to Ammut. But most traditions do not depict their judges as being so kindly. The Native American Hopi tradition says that when a wicked person dies, a witch known as a "Two Heart" comes for him and leads him away to the country of the witches, which is just as wicked as the people themselves were in life.[1]

The Hindu tradition is even more fearsome. Yama is the Hindu god of death. He is a fearful character, and is the one to whom the duty of judging the dead falls in this tradition. As Alaine Danélou describes him,

Yama owns two four-eyed dogs with wide nostrils, who were born to the Fleet-One (Sarama), the bitch who guards the herds of Indra. They watch the path of the dead.

When the soul leaves the body, the messengers of Yama lead the tired being through a barren district without shade or water till he reaches the city of Yama. There the dead ones go alone without friends or family. Their deeds accompany them. After the record-keeper, Citragupta, has read an account of the dead man's actions, kept in a book called Main Records, the soul is brought to receive its sentence before the throne of Yama, who appears gracious to the just, fearful to the evildoers.

The sinners, entering from the southern gate, have to pass a gate of red-hot iron and cross the fetid and boiling river Abandonment, filled with blood, hair, and bones, and peopled with fearful monsters.

...To the sinner his limbs appear three hundred leagues long. His eyes are deep wells. His lips are thin, the color of smoke, fierce. He roars like the ocean of destruction. His hairs are gigantic reeds, his crown a burning flame. The breath from his wide nostrils blows off the forest fires. He has long teeth. His nails are like winnowing baskets.... He rides the buffalo Fearful. His hands are like claws.[2]

Yama is also the name of the King of Hell in the Chinese Taoist tradition, and his love of suffering is legend. In the Treatise on Response and Retribution a story is told of a man named Fan Ki, who led an evil life, and sowed disharmony wherever he went. He died suddenly, but a day later he came back to life and called his family and neighbors together to address them. He told them that he had visited the Land of the Dead, and its King had told him, "This is where those who have died are punished for their wickedness. The living do not know what is in store for them. They will be tossed onto a bed of coals, the heat of which is in direct proportion to the extent of the evil they have done."

His family and neighbors just thought he was crazy, and refused to believe it. Fan Ki heard the voice of the King of the Dead, and doing as it commanded, he plunged a knife into his torso, crying out, "This is my punishment for encouraging people to live evil lives." He stabbed out both of his eyes, shouting, "This is in punishment for looking with rage upon my parents, and at women with lust." He sliced off his right hand, saying, "This is for all the animals I have killed," he cut open his chest and pulled out his own heart, crying out, "This is my punishment for causing others to be tortured." Then he cut out his tongue for lying and slandering others.

People from far and wide heard about this display, and came to see it for themselves. Fan Ki's family was horrified and tried to stop them, but Fan Ki croaked, "Let them come. The King of Death has sent me as a warning—who are you to stop me from my task?" He rolled on the floor in agony for six days, at which time he finally died.[3]

The God of Judgment in Abrahamic Religions

Judaism's God is not, by and large, an other-worldly being, nor concerned with any world but this one. The judgment pronounced by Yahweh was reserved only for those on earth, and concerned with the apostasy of the living and the consequences, if not to the perpetrators, then to their descendants.

No sooner had God rescued the children of Israel from slavery than he threatened to destroy them, for the simple "crime" of creating an image through which to worship "him," which is, by the way, the only way they knew how to worship at the time, as the Egyptians made extensive use of idols (Ex. 32). Moses intercedes, saying, "O Lord, why does your wrath burn hot against your people, whom you brought out of the land of Egypt with great power and with a mighty hand? Why should the Egyptians say, 'It was with evil intent that he brought them out to kill them in the mountains, and to consume them from the face of the earth'? Turn from your fierce wrath; change your mind and do not bring disaster on your people. Remember Abraham, Isaac, and Israel, your servants, how you swore to them by your own self, saying to them, 'I will multiply your descendants like the stars of heaven, and all this land that I have promised I will give to your descendants, and they shall inherit it forever.'" And the Lord changed his mind about the disaster that he planned to bring on his people."

In an example seen as prophesying the Diaspora, God promised to scatter Israel among the nations of the world from one end to the other for their unfaithfulness:

> The LORD will scatter you among all peoples, from one end of the earth to the other; and there you shall serve other gods, of wood and stone, which neither you nor your ancestors have known. Among those nations you shall find no ease, no resting place for the sole of your foot. There the LORD will give you a trembling heart, failing eyes, and a languishing spirit. Your life shall hang in doubt before you; night and day you shall be in dread, with no assurance of your life (Deut. 28:64-66, NRSV).

The Hebrew scriptures are filled with portentous warnings of how God would abandon his people to their enemies if they did not do as he commanded. A typical example is found in Second Kings:

> They despised his statutes, and his covenant that he made with their ancestors, and the warnings that he gave them. They went after false idols and became false; they followed the nations that were around them, concerning whom the LORD had commanded them that they should not do as they did. They rejected all the commandments of the LORD their God and made for themselves cast images of two calves; they made a sacred pole, worshiped all the host of heaven, and served Baal. They made their sons and their daughters pass through fire; they used divination and augury; and they sold

themselves to do evil in the sight of the LORD, provoking him to anger. Therefore the LORD was very angry with Israel and removed them out of his sight; none was left but the tribe of Judah alone. Judah also did not keep the commandments of the LORD their God but walked in the customs that Israel had introduced. The LORD rejected all the descendants of Israel; he punished them and gave them into the hand of plunderers, until he had banished them from his presence (II Kings 17:15-20).

Such thinking is not limited to ancient times. In the twentieth century, Rabbi Yoel Moshe Teitelbaum asserted that the sins of the Zionists were to blame for Hitler's execution of six million Jews.[5]

Judaism briefly flirted with ideas of Hell and judgment during and directly after their Babylonian exile, evidence of which can be found in the apocryphal and pseudepigraphal writings. Harwood points out that although Jesus spoke of permanent torture in Hell, such teaching "belongs strictly to Christian mythology. It has never been a part of the mythology of the Jews."[6]

In Jesus' teaching, God's wrath, while still capable of striking the living, had shifted its focus to the afterlife. The threat became not temporal destruction, but eternal torment. As Mackey points out, only once did Jesus speak of the God of Wrath exacting "his" vengeance in this world: "For great distress shall be upon the earth and wrath upon this people; they will fall by the edge of the sword, and be led captive among all nations; and Jerusalem will be downtrodden by the Gentiles, until the time of the Gentiles are fulfilled" (Luke 21:23b-24, RSV).

Mackey continues,

There is a more pronounced eschatological tone to God's "vengeance" in the New Testament. God's saving action is now centered in Christ and he frequently casts judgment in terms of eternal life—it is more closely associated with the possibility of Heaven or Hell. In the New Testament there is a shift from the nation Israel as the recipient of divine wrath to the individuals who reject God.[6]

In the Christian scriptures, it is Jesus himself who is the God of Judgment. One of the most famous judgment scenes appears in the Gospel of St. Matthew, where Jesus says,

> "...I was naked and you gave me clothing, I was sick and you took care of me, I was in prison and you visited me." Then the righteous will answer him, "Lord...when was it that we saw you a stranger and welcomed you, or naked and gave you clothing? And when was it that we saw you sick or in prison and visited you?" And the king will answer them, "Truly I tell you, just as you did it to one of the least of these who are members of my family, you did it to me." Then he will say to those at his left hand, "You that are accursed, depart from me into the eternal fire prepared for the devil and his angels; for I was hungry and you gave me no food, I was thirsty and you gave me nothing to drink, I was a stranger and you did not welcome me, naked and you did not give me clothing, sick and in prison and you did not visit me." Then they also will answer, "Lord, when was it that we saw you hungry or thirsty or a stranger or naked or sick or in prison, and did not take care of you?"[7]

So that's how people get to Hell. But what is it like once they get there? In the Gospel of Mark, Jesus describes the conditions of the less-popular afterlife, saying,

> If your hand causes you to stumble, cut it off; it is better for you to enter life maimed than to have two hands and to go to hell, to the unquenchable fire. And if your foot causes you to

stumble, cut it off; it is better for you to enter life lame than to have two feet and to be thrown into Hell. And if your eye causes you to stumble, tear it out; it is better for you to enter the kingdom of God with one eye than to have two eyes and to be thrown into Hell, where their worm never dies, and the fire is never quenched. For everyone will be salted with fire.[8]

Hell and judgment are not just for people. Indeed, according to Christian mythology, the abode of the damned was originally intended only for Satan and his angels. It was only after God discovered that people would be willful and disobedient that "he" decided it would be the final resting place for rebellious human creatures as well. The book of Revelation describes the final end of Satan, and all that he has succeeded in deceiving,

They marched up over the breadth of the earth and surrounded the camp of the saints and the beloved city. And fire came down from heaven and consumed them. And the devil who had deceived them was thrown into the lake of fire and sulfur, where the beast and the false prophet were, and they will be tormented day and night forever and ever. Then I saw a great white throne and the one who sat on it; the Earth and the heaven fled from his presence, and no place was found for them. And I saw the dead, great and small, standing before the throne, and books were opened. Also another book was opened, the Book of Life. And the dead were judged according to their works, as recorded in the books. And the sea gave up the dead that were in it, Death and Hades gave up the dead that were in them, and all were judged according to what they had done. Then Death and Hades were thrown into the lake of fire. This is the second death, the lake of fire; and anyone whose name was not found written in the Book of Life was thrown into the lake of fire.[9]

For those of us who are used to thinking of Jesus' God being much more a God of love than that portrayed in the Hebrew scriptures, this shift of focus is disconcerting. God's wrath is that much more terrible in the Christian scriptures by virtue of its relentlessness and longevity. As Harwood writes,

> The most vicious portrayal of his God as a vengeful psychopath was painted by Jesus.... To this day, Christians are reminded to "Fear God" and to beware of Jesus' eternal torture chamber where Yahweh condemns taboo-breakers to be slowly barbequed by flamethrowers and eaten by a worm that never dies. And this penalty is imposed, not only on hurters, persons who assault, kill and steal, but also on persons who, in an age of fully effective birth control, share joy.... [for] the Head Christian himself [the Pope], as a reward for attempting to murder the entire human species by forcing it to overpopulate itself into starvation and extinction, will be given the privilege of watching them burn.[10]

The God of Judgment is described in a relatively small percentage of the Christian scriptures, but the subsequent tradition has, at various stages, focused upon the fate of the wicked at length and with great relish. The following passage from James Joyce's *The Portrait of the Artist as a Young Man*, while somewhat lengthy, is worth quoting in that it is remarkable in it's capturing the spirit of hellfire and damnation preaching so prevalent in the Christian tradition since the enlightenment—and very similar to many sermons I myself grew up hearing:

> Hell is a strait and dark and foul-smelling prison, an abode of demons and lost souls, filled with fire and smoke.... In earthly prisons the poor captive has at least some liberty of movement, were it only within the four walls of his cell or in the gloomy yard of his prison. Not so in Hell. There, by reason

of the great number of the damned, the prisoners are heaped together in their awful prison the walls of which are said to be four thousand miles thick: and the damned are so utterly bound and helpless that, as a blessed saint, Anselm writes...they are not even able to remove from the eye a worm that gnaws it.

They lie in exterior darkness. For, remember, the fire of Hell gives forth no light. As, at the command of God, the fire of the Babylonian furnace lost its heat but not its light, so at the command of God, the fire of Hell, while retaining the intensity of its heat, burns eternally in darkness. It is a never-ending storm of darkness, dark flames and dark smoke of burning brimstone, amid which the bodies are heaped one upon the other without even a glimpse of air....

The horror of this strait and dark prison is increased by its awful stench. All the filth of the world, all the offal and scum of the world, we are told, shall run there as to a vast reeking sewer when the terrible conflagration of the last day has purged the world. The brimstone too which burns there in such prodigious quantity fills all Hell with its intolerable stench: and the bodies of the damned themselves exhale such a pestilential odor that, as saint Bonaventure says, one of them alone would suffice to infect the whole world. The very air of this world, that pure element, becomes foul and unbreathable when it has been long enclosed. Consider then what must be the foulness of the air of Hell. Imagine some foul and putrid corpse that has lain rotting and decomposing in the grave, a jellylike mass of liquid corruption. Imagine such a corpse a prey to flames, devoured by the fire of burning brimstone and giving off dense choking fumes of nauseous loathsome decomposition. And then imagine this sickening stench, multiplied a million fold and a million fold again from the millions upon millions of fetid carcasses massed together in the reeking darkness, a huge and rotting human fungus. Imagine all this and you will have some idea of the horror of the stench of Hell.

But this stench is not, horrible though it is, the greatest physical torment to which the damned are subjected. The torment of fires is the greatest torment to which the tyrant has ever subjected his fellow creatures.... The lake of fire in Hell is boundless, shoreless, and bottomless... . And this terrible fire will not afflict the bodies of the damned only from without but each lost soul will be a hell unto itself, the boundless fire raging in its very vitals. O, how terrible is the lot of those wretched beings! The blood seeths and boils in the veins, the brains are boiling in the skull, the heart in the breast glowing and bursting, the bowels a redhot mass of burning pulp, the tender eyes flaming like molten balls....

Every sense of the flesh is tortured and every faculty of the soul therewith: the eyes with impenetrable utter darkness, the nose with noisesome odors, the ears with yells and howls and execrations, the taste with foul matter, leprous corruption, nameless suffocating filth, the touch with red-hot goads and spikes, with cruel tongues of flame. And through the several torments of the senses the immortal soul is tortured eternally in its very essence amid the leagues upon leagues of glowing fires kindled in the abyss by the offended majesty of the Omnipotent God and fanned into everlasting and ever-increasing fury by the breath of the anger of the Godhead.[11]

The God of Judgment in the Christian tradition brings with it another shift: the measure of righteousness is no longer one's deeds, but one's beliefs. Hell is reserved not for those who do wicked things, but for those who do not subscribe to the peculiar dogmas of those in ecclesial power.

But the God of Judgment described in the Christian scriptures is tame in comparison to that found in the Koran, if only due to the sheer volume of references. Indeed, the author of the Koran seemed to derive unending delight from meditating on the fate of the wicked in the afterlife, since more than two thirds of each of the Koran's chapters have sections devoted to Hell and the fate of unbelievers. According to Izutsu, the pivotal point of the Koran is "the eschatological concept of the Day of Judgment, with God Himself presiding over everything as the stern, strict, and righteous judge, before whom men stand only in silence with bowed heads. The image of this decisive day should be held up constantly before the eyes of men in such a way that it might lead them to absolute earnestness, instead of levity and carelessness, in life. This is the dominant note of the Islamic piety."[12]

The most difficult task has not been assembling passages to illustrate this point from the Koran, but selecting amongst them judiciously, so as not to overwhelm the reader. Following is an assortment indicative of the spirit pervasive throughout the Koran:

Have you heard of the Event which will overwhelm mankind? On that day there shall be downcast faces, of men broken and worn out, burnt by a scorching fire, drinking from a seething fountain. Their only food shall be bitter thorns, which will neither sustain them nor satisfy their hunger (88:1-2).

When the earth shakes and quivers and the mountains crumble away and scatter abroad into fine dust, you shall be divided into three multitudes: those on the right (blessed shall be those on the right!); those on the left (damned shall be those on the left!); and those to the fore (foremost shall be those!)…. As for those on the left hand (wretched shall be those on the left hand!) they shall dwell amidst scorching winds and seething water: in the shade of pitch-black smoke, neither cool nor refreshing. For they have lived in comfort and persisted in the heinous sin, saying: "When we are once dead and turned to dust and bones, shall we, with all our forefathers, be raised to life?" Say: "This present generation, as well as the generations that passed before it, shall be brought together on an appointed day. As for you sinners who deny the truth, you shall eat the fruit of the Zaqqum-tree and fill your bellies with it. You shall drink boiling water: yet you shall drink it as the thirsty camel drinks." Such shall be their fate on the Day of Reckoning (56:2, 39-56).

This picture is grim, indeed, yet there are few passages in all of the world's religions which are as chilling as the following:

Each soul shall come attended by one who will testify against it and another who will drive it on. One of them will say: "Of this you have been heedless. But now we have removed your veil. Today you sight is keen." And his comrade will say: "My testimony is ready." Then a voice will cry: "Cast into Hell every hardened unbeliever, every opponent of good works, and every doubting transgressor who has set up another God besides Allah. Hurl him into the fierce, tormenting flames!" His companion will say: "Lord, I did not mislead him. He was already gone far astray." Allah will say: "Do not dispute in My presence. I gave you warning beforehand. My word cannot be changed, nor am I unjust to My servants." On that day We shall ask Hell: "Are you full?" And Hell will answer: "Are there any more?" (50:21-30).

And as in the Christian scriptures, descriptions of the actual, physical environment of Hell, and the tortures of its inhabitants, abound:

The damned shall be cast into the fire of Hell, where, groaning and wailing, they shall abide as long as the heavens and the earth endure, unless your Lord ordains otherwise (11:105-7).

The fruit of the Zaqqum-tree shall be the sinner's food. Like dregs of oil, like scalding water, it shall simmer in his belly. A voice will cry: "Seize him and drag him into the depth of Hell. Then pour out boiling water over his head, saying: 'Taste this, illustrious and honorable man! This is the punishment which you doubted'" (44:46-47).

For the wrongdoers We have prepared a fire which will encompass them like the walls of a pavilion. When they cry out for drink they shall be showered with water as hot as molten brass, which will scald their faces. Evil shall be their drink, dismal their resting-place (18:30).

Would that you knew what this is like! It is a scorching fire (101:1-11).

The only thing more horrifying than the descriptions of the tortures that await the damned in the Abrahamic traditions is the glee with which the true believers of those faiths look forward to the final judgment. It reveals the sadistic underbelly of related traditions that revel in the anticipated pain of those who are "other," and inverts the categories of "the righteous" and "the wicked" in the estimation of any humane, feeling person.

Further confounding is the headlong rush to hasten the day of judgment amongst Christian Zionists, who are doing everything in their power to fulfill every aspect of biblical prophesy which, in their interpretation, must occur before the Second Coming. Do not be mistaken: "Jesus is coming!" is not a shout of joy. It is a cry of revenge, a call to arms at which "the righteous" are quickened in their bloodlust, and lick their lips in sadistic anticipation of the senseless and horrifying suffering of others.

Then God, if he be good,
is not the author of all things,
as the many assert,
but he is the cause of a few things only,
and not of most things that occur to men....
The good is to be attributed to God alone;
of the evils the causes are to be
sought elsewhere, and not in him.

Plato

Chapter Seven

The Shadow of God

As a Christian fundamentalist, I lived in a world populated by demons and controlled by Satan. Every perceived evil was blamed on him, from the natural cycles of death and decay, to natural ways of being, such as skin color and sexual orientation. Anything that did not square with our sect's peculiar notions of what God intended was Satan's fault, and we were all his dupes if we dared to think otherwise.

Ours was a world where demons lurked around every corner. Every thought, every passing notion that did not square with our professed orthodoxy was rejected as a heresy that occurred to us as a result of demonic oppression. We understood that God would win in the end, but it was Satan who pulled the strings in the here and now. We cowered before his might, and prayed for deliverance from his deceptions and his power. Satan was raised up in our imaginations to be a much more powerful member of the Christian pantheon than even God was. Sure, we'd never admit as much, and intellectually we would balk at the idea, but we actually lived as if that were the case. We were functional Satanists, giving lip service to God, but ironically affording God's Enemy much more power over our lives than we did God "himself."

How did such a backwards and insidious way of life come about? When did we simply hand our souls over to Evil? The answer is, when we stopped believing God "himself" was the evil one.

As has been made abundantly clear so far in this book, the gods (and, later, God) never had a very stellar record as far as being a "nice guy." The polytheistic gods were unapologetically fallible, and just as hedonistic, cruel, and corrupt as humans ever were. Even as the idea of the One God emerged in ancient Israel, this God was likewise the source of both evil and good. But as humans developed ethically, such moral ambivalence in divinity became more and more of a problem. How could it be that humans were morally superior to their own maker?

Increasingly uncomfortable with the darker aspects of divinity, people naturally began searching for other explanations. God, demanding righteousness from "his" people, began to "feel" the expectation of reciprocity. If God demands righteousness, then God must be righteousness par excellence (never mind that the record contradicts such a notion). One way to address the problem was to split the beneficent and horrific sides of God into separate entities, thus keeping the "good" God unsullied by more unsavory behaviors, and creating a divine scapegoat upon which to pin the naughty behaviors. The idea caught on, and if the popularity of "deliverance" revivals of evangelical Protestantism are any indication, it is one likely to remain with us for some time.

When the person of Satan first appears in Judaic literature, he is not a bad guy at all. In fact, he is quite clearly on God's payroll. The word "satan" means, in Hebrew, "adversary," and he is repeatedly employed for God's own designs. In an early appearance in the book of Numbers we read of the King of Moab in great distress over the coming people of Israel on their way to Canaan. The King sent for a prophet named Balaam, who was famous for his efficacious blessings and curses. Balaam got on his donkey and headed for Moab, but, we are told, "God's anger blazed at him for going, and the Lord's angel placed himself on the road as an adversary against him" (Num. 22:6).

The "adversary" angel is the one responsible for convincing David to take the census — a test which he apparently failed, since

God later punishes him for it. During the exilic period, Zechariah writes, "Then he showed me the high priest Joshua confronted by the angel of Yahweh. And the Adversary was standing by, in order to accuse him, but the angel of Yahweh said to the Adversary 'Yahweh rebuke you, O Adversary! Yes, Yahweh who delights in Jerusalem rebuke you! Is not this man a charred stick pulled out of the fire'?" Ivor Morrish comments that this passage "would seem to indicate the role played by the Satan in the heavenly court. He is not yet seen...as the epitome of Evil, but rather as one whose function it is to accuse individuals before God, and to demonstrate their unworthiness of God's attention and divine consideration."[1] Satan's role in this stage of Judaism appears to be as the prosecuting attorney in the heavenly court. Satan appears in a very similar role in the book of Job.

The idea that there is a demonic power that is opposed to divinity first arose in ancient Persia with the prophet Zoroaster. God was known to the prophet as Ahura Mazda, who reigned over an elaborate hierarchy of angelic beings. Zoroaster beheld the goodness of life as being the gift of Ahura Mazda, but also that this life was beset on all sides by corruption and evil. Says Zoroastrian scholar Rustom Masani, "The Sage of Iran furnished a solution of this mystery by positing two primeval powers at war with each other. One of these Principles is called Spenta Mainyu, the Beneficent Spirit, and the other Angra Mainyu, the Evil Spirit."[2]

Thus, Zoroastrianism was not originally a true dualism, as Angra Mainyu is not the opposite of the One God, Ahura Mazda, but of Spenta Mainyu, the "Holy Spirit." Masani explains:

Spenta Mainyu [is] the son of Ahura Mazda, the first in the creation, occupying the first place in the celestial hierarchy. It is through him that the Prophet longs to approach Ahura Mazda, and it is through him that the human mind receives divine illumination. Good thoughts proceed from him, and good words and good deeds are the outcome of good thoughts. At the opposite pole stands Angra Mainyu, the Evil Spirit, who introduces discord and death in the world. The daevas, the offspring of the Evil Spirit, have chosen him as their lord; and he teaches them to mislead man through evil thought, evil word, or evil deed, and to lure him by his wiles to the path of wickedness. Whoever falls a victim to Angra Mainyu finds his thoughts enslaved by him. Man must avoid him as he would a pestilence. The best way to avoid the Evil Spirit is to think of and to espouse the cause of the Good Spirit. It is only when man's mind is not filled with good thoughts...that it becomes an easy prey to Angra Mainyu.[3]

These two spirits, Spenta Mainyu and Angra Mainyu, were believed to be polar opposites in every way. According to the ancient Zoroastrian scriptures, the Gathas, Spenta Mainyu tells Angra Mainyu, "Never shall our minds harmonize, nor our doctrines; neither our aspirations, nor yet our beliefs; neither our words, nor yet our deeds; neither our hearts, nor yet our souls."[4] Not surprisingly the distinction between Spenta Mainyu and Ahura Mazda eventually blurred, until Angra Mainyu (also known as Ahriman) came to be thought of as Ahura Mazda's equal and opposite power.

It was not until Israel was taken captive into Persia, where they encountered the Zoroastrianism of their captors, that the notions of angels and demons as we now know them entered the Jewish imagination. "The conception of the Evil Spirit," writes Masani, "was also influenced by the belief in the existence of Angra Mainyu. Asmodeus, who figures in the apocryphal book of Tobit, is positively the Mazdean wrath-demon Aeshma Deava."[5] Other notions, such as the immortality of the soul, the resurrection of the body, and future reward and punishment are also Zoroastrian bequests to the Jewish mythos.[6]

Such notions were later seen as inauthentic additions to the

Jewish tradition, and relegated to the category of folklore and myth. But in the period when these ideas were current and widely taught, another tradition rose up from within Judaism that would make these ideas foundational to its theology. I am speaking, of course, of Christianity, and the partial dualism of early Zoroastrianism is a strong element in most Christian writings.

Satan was a full-fledged mythological figure in Jesus' time. Early in his ministry, he was driven into the wilderness where Satan himself met and tempted him to turn aside from his mission (Lk. 4:13). Satan was spoken of as the scapegoat that keeps unbelievers in blindness (2 Cor. 4:3-4). He was the father of lies (John 8:44), and sometimes may appear "as an angel of light" (2 Cor. 11:14). The end of the book of Revelation describes in detail the binding of Satan (eliminating his power) and his final end in the Lake of Fire, his final home which he will share with all those who have been duped by his wiles.

Harwood writes,

Before the end of the first century...Satan was viewed as the eternal enemy of Christ the Lord, the Son of Man, and the Servant of Yahweh. The binding of the Prince of Darkness is seen ultimately as the only effectual way of destroying the power of evil over the world, the Cosmos, and the redeemed. The "dark twin," the Prince of Darkness—whatever he may be named in historical time, and however he may be described in human terms—has to be conquered once and for all by the "light twin," the Light of the World and Prince of Peace, in order that the very universe itself may be purified.[7]

This role is similar to the original ideas of Zoroaster, Jesus and Satan being the equal and opposite forces as were Spenta Mainyu and Angra Mainyu, reserving the top rank for Ahura Mazda, or Yahweh. Just as the esteem of Angra Mainyu grew in

Zoroastrianism, Satan's power grew to rival God's in Christian thought. Paul calls Satan "the god of this world," (2 Cor. 4:4) and the first epistle of Peter pictures him as a roaring lion, "seeking whom he may devour" (5:8).

Soon after, the radical dualism of the Gnostics began to make its appearance, in whose mythos the grand culprit became Yahweh himself. The Gnostics declared that the Hebrew God was a pretender to the throne, a vile demiurge who wished to keep the inhabitants of this planet enslaved. Far away was the true God, whose spark was in each human being, and to whom each soul longed to return. Jacques Lacarriere describes the beliefs of one early Gnostic who actually makes an appearance in the book of Acts, Simon Magus:

> How does God spend his time? Persecuting man and the human race. He creates Adam, then Eve, set them down in Paradise, but immediately forbids them the one essential: knowledge of Good and Evil. After this, and having chased the first human couple out of Paradise, he hounds their descendants unremittingly, multiplying the laws of prohibition, threatening the human species with the lightning of his wrath until the day when, with the Flood, he will wipe them out. But still it is not enough, and once again he showers the second humanity, the children of Noah, with fire, blood, and calamity. He is a God of justice, a cosmic Policeman whose intransigent authoritarianism antagonizes even the angels, and who never intervenes in earthly matters except to thwart human evolution.
>
> In arguing thus, Simon does not question or doubt the reasons for this aggressive behavior. He does not deny man's errors or his crimes, but declares simply that this image of an avenging God, ruthlessly hammering mankind, is incompatible with the idea of a good God, the friend of man and creator of life. From this he concludes that since this world and

this humanity, inaugurated in blood and crime, are patently the work of Jehovah, the latter cannot be the true God, but is a false God or simply a demiurge, that sadistic and perverse demiurge depicted in the Bible as a touchy, vindictive, choleric, jealous, and evil being.[8]

Another early heterodox christian, Marcion, viewed Yahweh in a similar manner, but believed the God of Jesus and the New Testament (a term Marcion coined, incidentally) was an altogether different deity. According to Blumenthal, Marcion believed that it was impossible "that Jesus, who is the Son of God, should be the Son of [Yahweh] the exterminator, or that the latter could be the Father whom Jesus claims. Marcion arrives at the same logical conclusion as Simon Magus: [Yahweh] is not the true God. The latter is the Unknown God, a stranger to this world, the true Father whose Son is Jesus Christ."[9]

For the Gnostic, human beings are "exploited on a cosmic scale, we are the proletariat of the demiurge-executioner, slaves exiled into a world that is viscerally subjected to violence; we are the dregs and sediment of a lost heaven, strangers on our own planet."[10] Our true home is with the God-whom-we-do-not-know, the God of whom Jesus brought us our first real knowledge.

In Islam, Satan's mythology takes another unexpected turn. According to the Koran, Satan, or Iblis, as he is called in Islam, falls because of his unflinching fidelity to Allah, and will not betray him even at the cost of his soul. The Koran tells us,

We created man from dry clay, from black molded loam, and before him Iblis from smokeless fire. Your Lord said to the angels: "I am creating man from dry clay, from black molded loam. When I have fashioned him and breathed of my spirit into him, kneel down and prostrate yourselves before him." All of the angels prostrated themselves, except Iblis. He refused to prostrate himself. "Iblis," said Allah, "why do you not prostrate yourself?"

Iblis replied, "I will not bow to a mortal created of dry clay, of black molded loam."

"Begone," said Allah, "you are accursed. My curse shall be on you till Judgment Day."

"Lord," said Iblis, "reprieve me till the Day of Resurrection."

He answered, "You are reprieved till the Appointed Day."

"Lord," said Iblis, "since you have led me astray, I will seduce mankind on earth: I will seduce them all, except those that faithfully serve you."

He replied, "This is the right course for Me. You shall have no power over my servants, except the sinners who follow you (15:29-7). ...Begone! Hell is your reward, and the reward of those that follow you. An ample reward it shall be. Rouse with your voice whomever you are able. Muster against them all your forces. Be their partner in the riches and in their offspring. Promise them what you will (Iblis promises only to deceive them). But over My true servants you shall have no power. Your Lord will be their all-sufficient Guardian" (17:60-67).

In this shocking account, because Iblis will not bow down to a mere mortal, but only to Allah, he is "tricked" into Allah's service, to tempt and deceive the unbelievers until the end of time, when Iblis shall say, "True was the promise which Allah made you. I too made you a promise, but did not keep it. Yet I had no power over you. I called you, and you answered me. Do not now blame me, but blame yourselves. I cannot help you, nor can you help me. I never shared your belief that I was Allah's equal" (14:22).

Also issuing from the Islamic part of the world is another fascinating perspective on the Evil One, ironically similar to the "functional Satanism" of my childhood faith. I am speaking of the Yezidis, a dwindling, but still practicing sect in Iran descended from Zoroastrian, Gnostic, and Islamic influences. They believe that though Good is the best, and will ultimately triumph, it is basically ineffectual in the world as it is. The only way to get anything done is to appeal to the Devil for aid, under the protection of "The Peacock Angel." The Yezidis are currently very perplexed in that they cannot seem to interest their young people in their traditions, and may be in danger of dying out.

True dualism is rare. Almost all faiths insist that although evil may be powerful, it is under the control of, or at least is far inferior to, a much higher deity. What is perplexing is that the projection of divine evil onto a "person" such as Satan does little to mitigate God's guilt in regards to evil in the world. In many cases, Satan is God's agent, his "ax-man," merely carrying out the malevolent will of the deity; and in others, God passively sits by and does nothing while Satan is given free reign in his terrors. Whether by sin of commission or omission, the proposition of the Devil does not ameliorate God of blame—it just makes for a more interesting story.

"If only I could fight with both my friends and foes,
Join in my ear God, anti-God, both yes and no
Like that round fruit which two lips make
when they are kissing!"

Nikos Kazentzakis

Chapter Eight

Talking Back to God

In many ways, I had a very happy childhood. My parents were not overly strict, I never went hungry, and I was well-provided for. But one very painful aspect of growing up in our house was this: while it was perfectly permissible for my parents to express anger, if my sister or I dared to express it, or even to hint at it, we would be surely punished. Consequently, I never learned how to hold my anger in a way that did not do internal damage. Instead of expressing it outwardly, I turned it inward, which resulted in a crippling depression. It was only after many years of psychotherapy that I learned how to express anger in healthy and empowering ways. Once I did, the depression, miraculously, lifted.

I have learned, through talking to many friends over the years, that my experience, while far from universal, is not that unusual. But it does seem to be a universal experience when considering the relationship between Christians and their "Heavenly Father." From nearly the beginning of Christian history, people have been taught to accept the church's dogma uncritically, deny the validity of their own experience, and ignore simple compassion and common sense. The idea of standing up to God, questioning God, or confronting God for "his" sins has always been unthinkable for Christians. The Christian family is a hopelessly dysfunctional one, with an abusive "Father" careening out of control at its head, and all the children too terrified of Hell to say "boo" about it. (If you don't agree with this estimation of God, you have clearly not been paying attention up to this point.)

The time for the Christian community to be content being cringing, perpetual children is past, and long overdue for change. Too many horrors have been wrought by God or in God's name for us to remain silent and compliant (and therefore complicitous) any longer. We would do well to learn from our spiritual forbears, the Jews, on this score, as they have a long history of standing up to God. Hugo Gryson tells the following story:

The rabbi is in his synagogue in a small village in Poland, at Yom Kippur—the Day of Atonement. And there is one man there, the tailor, who is apparently having the most dreadful argument—shaking his fists and muttering and everybody is disturbed by it but nobody likes to interrupt the service. But when it ends, the rabbi turns to this man and says, "My friend, what on earth was going on there?"

"Ah!" says the tailor, "I got into a terrible argument with God. I said to Him, 'Look, I know I am not perfect. There have been times when I sat down and had my meal without saying the blessing or the grace. And there have been days when I have hurried through my prayers. And to confess it, I have occasionally charged people for double thread when I only used single, and sometimes I have kept a bit of cloth back to make clothes for my own children. So I'm not claiming any special privileges. But you, God! You take babies away from their mothers. Young men die on the field of battle. People are cut down before their time through illness. How can you let this happen? So let me make a bargain with you. If you'll forgive me, I'll forgive you.'"

And the tailor says to the rabbi, "Did I do wrong?" And the rabbi answers the tailor, "My friend, you had such a strong case—why did you let God off so easily?"[1]

The book of Job is a brilliant analysis of this very problem. Trying to understand why so many terrors have beset Job, his friends — assuming a just and righteous deity — pin the blame on Job himself. This is typical of attitudes even today in cases of domestic abuse: the victim is made to feel that the violence is somehow her (or his) fault, or a person's religious community convinces the victim that the present violence is just reward for past sins — Job's predicament precisely. Hence, according to Marie F. Fortune,

> A battered woman now being abused by her husband can "explain" why this is happening by remembering that when she was sixteen, she had sexual intercourse once with her boyfriend. She knows this was a "sin" and that God was displeased with her, so God must now be punishing her teenage indiscretion. Or she may have been "disobedient" and not submitted to her husband. She understands the situation to reflect God's acting to bring about her suffering for a justifiable reason; she blames herself and accepts her battering as God's will for her. At least she can "explain" why this happened to her; unfortunately, her explanation leaves no room for questioning her suffering or for confronting her abuser with his responsibility for it.[2]

Job, on the other had, does confront his abuser, as quixotic a proposition as that might seem. According to Blumenthal, Job "never questions God's existence, nor God's power to do what God is doing. Rather, Job questions God's justification, God's morality, God's justice."[3] He rejects the theological rationalizations of the people around him (as does God), and, while remaining loyal to God, calls him on the carpet for his trespasses. Job says to his friends,

> How long will you aggravate me and oppress me with words?

Ten times you have humiliated me; are you not ashamed that you have dealt harshly with me?...Know now that it is God who has twisted me, who has cast his net upon me. I shout "Violence!" but I am not answered. I cry out but there is no fairness. He has blocked my way; I cannot pass.... My skin and flesh cling to my bones, and I am left with only my skull.... For I know that my Redeemer is alive and, though he be the last being in the universe, when the period of my abuse is at an end, all this shall be struck away and then, from my body, I shall see God, whom I once envisioned, whom my eyes once saw, and who was not strange to me (Job 19, excerpts).

Psychologist Carl Jung comments,

"It is Yahweh himself who darkens his own counsel.... He turns the tables on Job and blames him for what he himself does: man is not permitted to have an opinion about him.... For seventy-one verses he proclaims his world-creating power to his miserable victim, who sits in ashes and scratches his sores with potsherds, and who by now has had enough of superhuman violence."[4]

The figure of Job has become more and more important in Jewish scholarship since the Holocaust, as the archetypal drama lived out by an entire people. Just as the Jews were in no way to blame for the hatred and genocide leveled against them, so they must come to grips with their God who stood idly by and allowed such atrocities to happen. Elie Wiesel, in his play "The Trial of God," explored this theme by trying God for the Cossack massacres in the Fourteenth Century. In it, Wiesel sums up what Blumenthal calls a "theology of protest":

If He insists upon going on with His methods, let Him—but I won't say Amen. Let Him crush me, I won't say Kaddish. Let

Him kill me, let Him kill us all, I shall shout and shout that it's His fault. I'll use my last energy to make my protest known. Whether I live or die, I submit to Him no longer.... And they kept quiet? Too bad—then I'll speak for them. For them, too, I'll demand justice.... To you, judges, I'll shout, "Tell Him what He should not have done: tell Him to stop the bloodshed now...." I lived as a Jew, and it is as a Jew that I die—and it is as a Jew that, with my last breath, I shall shout my protest to God! And because the end is near, I shall shout louder! Because the end is near, I'll tell Him that He's more guilty than ever![5]

How do we deal with such a God? How do we deal with the monster, the shadow of the very one who gives and sustains our life? What kind of God allows six million of "his" beloved to be exterminated? What kind of God can simply stand by as grievous injustices that "he" could alleviate are being perpetrated—sometimes in "his" own name? "How could a supreme God have conceived the incredible sequences, mechanisms, massacres, and annihilations that constitute the very practice of life itself?" asks Lacarriere. "What warped mind could have invented the procreative act of the praying mantis.... What immeasurable sadistic being could have thought up the paralyzing sting of the ammophilous wasp, which it sticks into the flesh of caterpillars, that they may be devoured alive by the larvae of the winged insect?"[6] And most especially, in Miller's words, "what is insufferable on the part of God...is to have invented a creature [humankind] who visits more suffering upon himself than inanimate nature can inflict. That, I think, is something for which God should be at Nuremberg."[7] How do we deal with such an entity?

David Blumenthal tells us that, "As the paradigmatic survivor of the Holocaust, Wiesel has let it be known that he, and hence we, cannot forgive God; nor can he, and hence we, be silent. He must let his voice ring out, he must protest; so must we."[8] This is the basis of Blumenthal's "theology of protest," which encourages us to look the abuser straight in the eye, and to speak the truth as we see it. The first step, says Blumenthal, is by "admitting that Scripture does indeed portray God as an abusing person."[9] We must resist the temptation to rationalize God's behavior, make excuses for it, or re-interpret the abusive scriptural testimony so as to make God's actions "easier to swallow." They are hard to swallow, and should stay that way. Baudler points out that "perhaps religion could help to master the experience of evil in human life more efficiently if this bull-like aspect of God, which crystallizes a concrete experience, were not pushed aside too quickly in favor of an abstract teaching in which God cannot be anything but good."[10]

A God which cannot be anything but good is a fantasy: it does not deal squarely with the facts of human experience, and it presents a simplistic and unrealistic worldview that cannot be maintained with integrity. Sontag says, "Tame Gods accept goodness easily, and no risk is involved for man. To accept evil into himself, however, requires a powerful God and also one with whom it is more dangerous for man to deal."[11] And also more realistic. If we are going to deal realistically and honestly with the problem of evil in human life, we must not ignore the problem of evil in God. Sontag continues,

A God who is merely pleasant is ruled out, and so is one who intends simply good things. The unpleasant and the destructive are his intentions too, although it is not impossible to account for them as serving some proposed ulterior motive... He must be capable of witnessing evil without being crushed by it, as we often are, since he sometimes allows it to overwhelm and to destroy us. We are led to a God who is not simply the fulfillment of our wishes, but is capable of ordering a world in which even good wishes are often blocked from being fulfilled. The God of our romantic dreams is too one-sided for any argument based upon atheism. Instead, we discover a God who combines and balances a number of forces, both good and malignant. If we meet a God who does not exempt the good man from destruction, darkness cannot be avoided in seeking such a God. If any light is to be thrown on this apparently dark side of God, it will be up to man to do so, since God has left this side of his nature in the shadows.[12]

Though Sontag argues elsewhere that the unity of various aspects of the divine supercede personality, I believe that the opposite is true. God possesses true personality precisely because "his" character is NOT one-dimensional. Like all persons, God is infinitely complex, possessed of the potential for both good and evil, and moved by psychological forces both philanthropic and pathological. God is sullied, and our choice is whether to live in denial of the facts with the God of our fantasies, or to be honest with ourselves, and deal with the God of our collective experience. Sontag comments on the necessity of this very complexity: "He is one powerful enough to control the added divergent forces which his complexity generates. Goodness alone, then, cannot lead to God nor can simplicity or unity if taken as exclusive guides. These are at best only partial clues and reveal only partial truths about God."[13]

How, then, do we approach the Monster God? Blumenthal says we must be very clear that the victims are not the guilty ones. God is responsible for God's own abuse. Second, it is only natural for the victim to distance him- or herself from the perpetrator. "We will think twice about whether we can, or even should approach God.... We will guard our distance — theologically and spiritually, in worship and in study."[14] Third, we must tell the truth. We must not hide the perpetrator or make excuses for "him." We will "cling tenaciously to our rage, and we will speak. And, in our speaking, we will accuse, we will place the blame where it belongs.... We will say, 'You are the abuser. The fault was yours. You repent. You return to us.'"[15] Fourth, we must get on with our lives and live them responsibly. Fifth, we must not abandon our spirituality, but affirm it.

Blumenthal explains that we accomplish the latter step by affirming,

> ...the grace of human contact and the sublimeness of the experience of the transcendent. And we will affirm the reality of God's presence, God's power, and even God's love — insofar as we have experienced these, or respect others who have. Ours will not be a self-effacing affirmation, nor a self-denying love; those days are gone. Rather, ours will be an acknowledgment of the Other Who is present to us in fear and in kinship, in terror and in presence.[16]

Another step we can take, says Elizabeth Bettenhausen, is by "refusing to be awed by violence, by refusing to grant it power." This will only be possible, she says, when we "refuse to cooperate in the ways of violence. No mother's blessing would attend her child's going off to war. No father's smile would greet the militaristic politician. No priest's pardon would hide the battering husband's sin.... No police policy would condone the rapist and condemn the woman."[17] And to this list we can add that no church member would look the other way when a fellow parishioner is being spiritually abused by a clergy person, and no person will be shamed out of their dignity by an abusive act of God.

Finally, we must not harden ourselves to the reality of God's goodness, "as painful as that is,"[18] and we must, in Blumenthal's words, "turn to address God, face to Face, presence to Presence."[19] The Rosh Hashana liturgy betrays how very long these ideas have been brewing in Judaism when it says,

May it be Your will, O Lord,
our God and God of our ancestors,
that Your prayer be fulfilled
that Your mercy defeat Your anger against us,
and that You repent before us,
in truth and with a whole heart;
for we are Your people and You are our God,
We are Your children and You are our Parent.[20]

The monstrosity of God is a reality we cannot avoid. What we can do is decide how we will be in relationship with such a God. Ignoring the evidence will not help us. Telling the stories, terrible though they may be, that we find in the Scriptures of the world is absolutely necessary if we are to confront the truth in ourselves, and confront God "himself." If we are brave enough to enter into this process, we will find a spiritual journey that is void of any easy answers, and a God who is, in spite of our best efforts to convince ourselves otherwise, all too human.

Listen! If all must suffer to pay for
[God's] eternal harmony,
what have children to do with it,
tell me, please?
It's beyond all comprehension
why they should suffer,
and why they should pay
for the harmony.

Fyodor Dostoevsky

Chapter Nine

The Search
for Another God

While not denying the need to look the abusing God square in the face, as discussed in the last chapter, I believe we also owe it to God to give "him" an opportunity for redemption. This is especially true since, for most of us, the experience of God is not monolithically pathological, but includes goodness, wisdom, and most appropriately for the business at hand, grace. Many of us are still alive because God has given us a second chance, and for those of us for whom this is true, God deserves no less.

I recognize the experience of the fundamentalism of my youth as one that was horribly abusive. I suffered under it myself, and I stood idly by and watched others suffer from it as well. More than this, I perpetuated this abuse by preaching the God of judgment to others. But as related in the introduction, my experience of God was redeemed by the discovery that the God I was given by my fundamentalist theological training was not the "real" God at all.

This is an intuition that goes all the way back to the Gnostics. According to the Gnostic Christian myth, the True God "gave birth" to many emanations, most of them existing in mated pairs. One of these emanations, Sophia, exited the Fullness (the pleroma in Greek) and found herself lost in chaos. Try as she might, she could not find her way back. So she tried to find God by imitating God. Since all God does is give birth to emanations, she gave birth to an emanation of her own. But because she reproduced without her mate (the Christ) the being she gave birth to was deformed. He was Samael, "the blind god."

Samael had never known any world but chaos, and like the divine being he was, he set about creating order. He made the earth, and surrounded it with his own emanations, the archons. Then he created Adam and Eve, and placed them within the garden. He told Adam and Eve that he was the one and only God, and that they must worship him alone. Then he instructed his archons to make sure that the souls of the humans could not escape, but to always return them to the earth in a perpetual cycle of reincarnation.

But Samael was blind because he knew nothing of the Fullness, the existence of the True God from whence Sophia emerged. Sophia took pity on Adam and Eve, and placed within them a spark of true divinity. Thus, there was a part of them that was greater than their creator, that longed to escape him and to return to the Fullness.

The True God also took pity on Adam and Eve, and sent Sophia's mate, the Christ, to inform them of their true situation. He came in the form of a serpent, and he told them that the being that created them was not the true God at all, but was merely a deluded pretender to the throne. When they heard this, their eyes were opened, and Samael's power over them was broken. The archons could not hold them captive when they died, and they were able to escape their clutches at death and enter into the bliss of the Fullness.

This myth was salvation itself when I first read it, for it showed me that the God I was given as a child was like Samael, a deluded pretender. And that there was another deity, a true God, beyond the evil of the fundamentalist system that called me to health and wholeness. Knowing this, I was liberated from the abusive power of the fundamentalist god, and was able to discover my true calling and destiny, even as Adam and Eve were.

The myth is very instructive for our purposes here, as well. For it may be that the gods to which our myths and traditions point are not the true God at all. There may be another God who is not horrific, who would not approve of the behavior of the monster gods. But if so, is it not truly "an unknown god"? If all of our spiritual sources of wisdom are deeply flawed, or in the service of malevolent deities, what sources do we have at our disposal to divine the nature of this true but unknown God?

Another View of Scripture

It may not be necessary to hastily discard our traditional sources of wisdom. I would like to suggest that the holy books of our various traditions are not, as many suppose, maps of reality as God sees it, but are flawed human records that describe the relationships between various peoples and the divine from an all-too-human perspective.

For all of the traditionalists' talk of "divine revelation" when it comes to their scriptures, no one argues against the fact that, at least on the surface, the texts were actually written by human beings. We can debate the level of "inspiration" these writers possessed, but the fingers that held the pens were, in every case, flesh and blood.

Like all human beings, they saw the world through the filters of their own understanding, their own cultures and prejudices, their own political realities, levels of social sophistication, and, most especially, their own dangerous exigencies. Regardless of the sincerity of their ideologies and commitment to the "truth" as they understood it, ultimately they could only understand it in terms that were familiar to them. Their own ideas were of necessity projected onto the Divine reality, inevitably coloring it, and at times rendering it utterly obscure.

Thus, as we saw in our first chapter, the fondness of the

Indians for their monarchies led them to project it onto the gods, creating Indra, the "king of the gods." The fear the Jews felt at being exterminated by their neighbors led them to understand their God's directives as calling for the utter annihilation of those neighbors. St. Paul's prejudice against homosexuals led him to believe that his opinion was shared by God, allowing him to promise hellfire for anyone who dared to follow his or her heart in this way.

These are the writings that traditionalists of every stripe label "inerrant," and "the Word of God." There may be something of the True God within them to be divined, but that truth must be discerned beneath layer after layer of cultural perspective, personal prejudice, and political projection. The idea that some agent of the divine was protecting such writings from error is absurd. For each claims this status only for their own scriptures (as if the Divine cares not at all for the health and salvation of "other" peoples), and none of these scriptures agree in any actual details (however much we may laud their "moral" or mystical similarities).

Not only do these writings not agree with one another, they are sorrowfully lacking in internal consistency as well. The Hindu tradition contains more creation myths than anyone can count, most of them mutually exclusive accounts. The Jewish record lays out two conflicting creation accounts side-by-side in the first and second chapters of Genesis (compare 1:1-2:3 with 2:4b-25), and in the Christian scriptures there are four stories of Jesus' resurrection in the four canonical gospels, none of which agree with one another and cannot be harmonized in a way that maintains the integrity of each account.

The Absurdity
of the Monster God

As we have painfully observed in the preceding chapters, it is very difficult to read the behaviors of these deities as recorded in their holy books as being anything but demonic. There is simply no way to logically argue their "holiness" from their actual scriptures.

I remember once, when counseling a woman who had been extremely wounded by her fundamentalist experience, I held her hand as she recounted the terror she felt trying to leave the fundamentalist church. Through her tears, she told me how scared she was of being cast into Hell for daring to question her church's theology. "Haven't you always been taught that God is your heavenly Father?" I asked her. She nodded and blew her nose. "Well, let's say you had a daughter. What if she did something really bad, let's say she killed somebody." She nodded, going along with my little thought experiment. "Would it be right for her to be punished for her crime?" She nodded that it was. "And what would an appropriate punishment be?"

She thought about it for a while, "I don't know, maybe twenty years in prison?"

"Shouldn't she be tortured for those twenty years?"

"No! Prison is enough."

"But the church says that just punishment for any sin is to be tortured in unthinkable agony, not for twenty years, but for all eternity. As a mother, would you allow your child to endure that if you had the power to stop it?"

"Of course not!"

"How does it feel to be morally superior to God?" I asked. She stopped in her tracks, and the utter and absurd ridiculousness of her fundamentalism confronted her head-on.

The traditionalists will, of course, argue that "God's ways are not our ways," and that it is impossible for humans to divine God's purposes or methods, and blasphemy to judge them. Yet the fact remains that if any human behaved as monstrously as the gods the traditionalists worship, we would have locked such deities up and thrown away the key a long time ago (or worse, were we in Texas). We could just as easily argue that we do not have the right to punish those humans whose ways we do not completely understand, yet that does not stop us from rendering guilty verdicts. What could possibly justify this divine immunity? What could inspire such loyalty for a criminal (other than the sheer terror of "his" retribution if we dared to be "disloyal")? What justifies our insistence on God's innocence despite such a mountainous assemblage of evidence to the contrary?

This may sound strange, but it may in fact be *love*. None of the humans we love are perfect. In fact, most of us are deeply flawed, and almost all of us have committed some variety of evil. Yet we love and are loved. And despite God's flaws, we manage to feel loved by God, and are moved to love "him" in return. The fact that such affection is not warranted is irrelevant—perhaps none of the affection we ourselves receive is warranted. Love is not rational. And just as many of us would sacrifice our lives to rescue another human being—even one we have never met—even so we are moved to sacrifice our rationality, our sense of justice, even our common sense, to rescue the honor of this one we call "God."

The Puzzle of Theodicy

Even if we are willing to explain away God's sins of commission as being the fiercesome projections of our traditions' mythmakers, we are left with the difficult puzzle of God's sins of omission. That God may go forth to slay sinners at the end of time by "his" own hand can be relegated to the revenge fantasies of the authors of scripture, but what are we to make of the omnipotent deity that sits idly by while Nazis exterminate millions of Jews? What of the complacency of the Divine who allows hundreds of thousands to starve to death as famine stretches from year to hungry year? What of the God who has the power to stop a tsunami in its tracks, but doesn't?

In our own system of justice, a person who witnesses a violent crime being committed and does not help (if he or she has the power to do so) is complicitous in the crime, and may be prosecuted as an accomplice. Yet why do we not hold God to this same standard of morality? A God who can rescue someone from suffering and death, but chooses not to is a criminal, plain and simple.

Theologians throughout the ages have concocted numerous strategies for dealing with this dilemma:

The *karmic defense* states that evil is visited upon humans because it is deserved. Either the gods allow people to suffer for evil they have committed in this life, as Job's friends accused, or in the case of those systems that believe in reincarnation, people suffer in this life as punishment for wrongs committed in previous lives.

Then there is the *free-will defense*, which argues that God must allow evil in the world, or otherwise humans' power to choose between good and evil would be mitigated, and the human project would fail. This may be a convincing argument as regards human evil, but does nothing to explain natural disasters.

Another option is the *soul-making defense*, first offered by St. Ireneaus in the third century, CE. This states that evil, both human and natural, must be suffered to exist for the purpose of human moral development. This seems logical on the surface, but the signal-to-noise ratio is simply too high – the good that results can in no way justify the amount of pain required.

A favorite amongst many religious folk is the *great reward defense*. This says that even though there is great suffering here, and that people often don't deserve it, it will all be okay in the end, because a great reward awaits them in heaven. For those enduring slavery, or who otherwise have no control over their situations, this can be a very great comfort indeed. But from an intellectual standpoint, it is pretty unfulfilling, for we must take on blind faith the existence of another life, and that it will be better than this one. This is one hell of a lot of faith.

Other theologians advocate the *mystery defense*. These "thinkers" simply throw up their hands and say, "We do not know the mind of God. We must trust 'his' wisdom and confess that it is a mystery." This has the benefit of at least being an honest approach — admitting as it does how very little we know — but it is otherwise intellectually lazy, and cannot satisfy the human need to make sense of the world.

The problem hangs upon a device that philosophers and theologians have called "the impossible triangle" (see figure, below). The impossible triangle has three points to it. One point is "God is all good," the next point is "God is all-powerful," and the final point is "Evil is real."

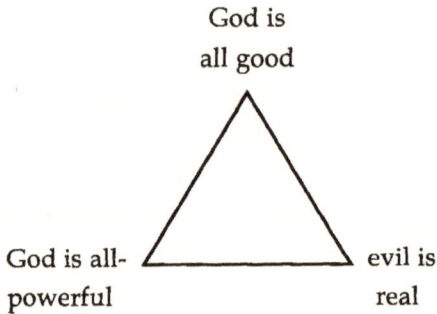

God is
all good

God is all-   evil is
powerful   real

The difficulty lies in the fact that one cannot hold all three points to be true and still be logically viable. If evil is a real and imminent danger, then a truly good God would not, nay, morally *cannot*, stand by and allow it to happen. And yet, evil happens all the time. David Hume asked the hard questions several centuries ago: "Is [God] willing to prevent evil, but not able? Then he is impotent. Is he able, but not willing? Then he is malevolent. Is he both able and willing? Whence, then, is evil?"

The impossible triangle was first formulated by the early Greek philosopher Epicurus, who wrote, "God is all-powerful. God is perfectly good. Evil exists. If God exists, there would be no evil. Therefore, God does not exist." Not all thinkers come to Epicurus' conclusion, of course. Various religious systems solve the problem of evil by opting out of one or more of the three points on the Impossible Triangle.

Hinduism, for instance, agrees that God is all powerful and God is all good, but denies the ultimate existence of evil. As such, it is a logically coherent system. The all-good and all-powerful deities of Hinduism do not need to eradicate evil, because it is not real in the first place. Evil, for Hindus, is an illusion. People only *seem* to suffer, but evil has no more reality than a Hollywood fiction. While this is a logical answer, it is not perfect, for it offers little comfort to the seemingly suffering, for whom the pain is very real indeed. Just try telling a man with a migraine, "Oh, it's okay, it doesn't *really* hurt!" or a mother who has just lost a child, "Stop crying! Your baby's not really dead, she was never really alive to begin with!" to see how much comfort this approach actually provides.

Another option is denying that God is all-good. All of the native traditions accept this view, as does early Judaism. The Gnostics certainly embraced this view, painting the creator of this world as being, at worst, a homicidal sociopath, and, at best, hopelessly inept. Unfortunately, this view flies in the face of our Platonic desire to keep God unsullied from the very urges that mar our own existence, but such sullying is not necessarily a bad thing. Why should God be perfect? What need does it address in us to project perfection—a fiction that resides nowhere in the phenomenal universe outside of the human imagination—onto God? What if God does not want—or deserve—to bear such a projected burden?

The final option is that God is not all-powerful. This is also a popular view amongst native traditions, but is not favored in Hinduism or monotheistic traditions. Again, what need does it address in human beings to project omnipotence onto divinity? Is existence just too scary to endure if there isn't a beneficent being who is ultimately in control? This is surely our stuff, then, not God's.

Many traditions do not fall neatly into these three categories, however. Taoism rejects all three points! For Taoists, there is ultimately no actual evil, God is not all-good, nor is God all powerful. Indeed, it is questionable whether one can say that Taoism posits a god at all. Many native traditions deny that their gods are all-good or all-powerful.

Most people are not likely to embrace the native traditions of their ancestors, however popular Wicca has become in recent years. But there is a viable monotheistic theology that also denies these two points. It emerged in the early twentieth century, has been taught to two generations of divinity students of every stripe, and has contributed to the emergence of such cutting-edge philosophical systems as Chaos Theory, Systems Theory, and the Gaia Principle. It is called Process Theology, and in it I believe we may discern the seeds of God's redemption.

A warning: Process Theology is not easy to grasp, and will take a lot of explaining. But if one is willing to make the intellectual investment, it is a very rewarding study indeed. And if one has any investment in a viable relationship with a God worth having, it is worth the effort. But you have been warned—if you dare to proceed, make sure your seatbelts are securely fastened. Reality is about to take a disorienting spin.

Process Theology

Process theology has its genesis in the teaching of the pre-socratic philosopher, Heraclitus, who taught that everything in the universe is in flux at all times. He said, "You can never step into the same river twice," because though you may be standing at the same spot on the riverbank, the water in a river is never the same water, as it is perpetually rushing by. So it is with all of being. Nothing is constant except perpetual change.

This kind of thinking popped up here and there throughout the history of philosophy, both East and West. But the next major contributor to what we think of as process thought today was George Frederick Hegel. Hegel's philosophy has its origins in a flash of mystical insight. He discerned that the universe was just one thing. This is a perspective common to mystics of every tradition, but not usually a popular starting point for philosophers.

Hegel's philosophy was the first critique of the "parts" mentality science has been so enamored of for centuries, now. While all around him scientists were breaking reality down into its constitutive elements Hegel warned us to take a step back and see the whole picture. "Only the whole is real," he wrote. Everything we are looking at must be seen in terms of its relationship to everything else, otherwise our view is distorted. This is a remarkably post-modern perspective, and resonates with many contemporary philosophies.

It is especially poignant when we consider God, for such a theory will not allow us to split God into different "parts," either! Hegel even provides us with a creation myth: In the beginning God was pure mind, pure being. Since God was alone, God attempted to think about "himself." (After all it was dreadfully dull, and as God was the only subject and the only object in existence, what else would God have to do?)

Unfortunately, the thought of pure being is impossible, apparently even for God, so when God tried to think about "himself," God thought about nothing instead.

Actually God thought about no-thing, the very opposite of being. But since God *is* God's thought, God's failure to comprehend "himself" resulted in an internal distance being created. Hegel calls this God's self-alienation.

We might see this self-alienation as the progenitor of Satan, in Western religion—God's self-alienated essence and the opposite of God's pure being. This alienation proved to be quite catastrophic for God, who has spent most of the life of the universe trying to reconcile God to "himself."

So what we have here is a God of two minds who can't seem to get it together. God can neither recapture the womb-like coziness of pure being, nor can God be content with annihilation.

All of history then falls somewhere in between, a vast space Hegel terms "becoming."

All the universe participates in this "becoming." In fact, the project of the universe is to re-acquaint God with God's self. Apparently, in trying to think about Godself, God lost "himself," and the whole vast drama of history is God's attempt to remember who God was. (Let that be a lesson to you not to be too self-absorbed.)

This is a kind of Western Hinduism — the universe exists only as a way for God to rediscover God's self. In Hinduism, however, this self-revelation is intentional and playful, but in Hegel's system, there is an element of desperation involved.

God's self-alienation is an extremely uncomfortable state for the almighty, and God is not only not playful, but is not at all happy about the situation. Not only that, but it is taking way too long to sort this little mess out. But according to Hegel, that is God's problem; for us, it's just the neighborhood we have to live in.

Hidden in this creation myth is Hegel's great gift to human thought, what we now call the "Hegelian dialectic." God's pure "being" was the thesis, God's subsequent thought of "no-thing" was the antithesis, and the resultant, ongoing process of "becoming" is the synthesis. This process, "thesis, antithesis, synthesis," Hegel subsequently applied to everything, from politics to history to religion, and in doing so he revealed history not as a static list of events but as a dynamic process in which every action is connected to the movement of the whole, every element is affected by every other element, and each event is formed and informed by those that have gone before it.

It is easy to see how helpful this insight was. Suddenly history made a whole lot more sense, and scientists in every discipline applied it to their studies with useful results.

Even when applied to our own smaller stories, the dialectic yields results. For instance, my own spiritual journey makes more sense when thought about in terms of Hegel's theory. I began my religious journey as a Southern Baptist, a denomination which stresses individualism and congregational polity. In college I was converted to catholicism, the very antithesis of my childhood faith in that it stresses communal life and is hierarchical in polity.

After many years, God led me to the parish I now serve, where thesis and antithesis have formed a synthesis we like to call "congregational catholicism," which preserves the best of both worlds, being both communal and self-governing — thesis, antithesis, synthesis.

One cannot take Hegel's creation myth too seriously, no more so than any other, but the dialectic it points to is invaluable. It paved the way for many more thinkers, chief of whom for our purposes here is the man who is generally thought of as the father of contemporary Process thought, Alfred North Whitehead.

Whitehead was a mathematician, who was offered a post in philosophy at Harvard even though he had never taken a single course in philosophy. One Harvard official was heard to quip, "The first philosophy course he ever attended was the one he taught." Whitehead's classes were very popular, but he was less popular amongst his colleagues, whom he horrified by daring to speculate about God.

In Whitehead's system, there are no things in the universe, only events, actions, or processes. Quantum mechanics has borne Whitehead's assertion out: solid matter is an illusion, and in reality there are only the actions of electrons, which are themselves actions leaping in and out of observability.

Whitehead prefers to speak of *becoming* rather than *being*. Everything we perceive is a process of becoming. Everything we understand as a thing, or as a being, Whitehead calls an *actual occasion*, or an *event*.

Whitehead is not at all an easy thinker to grasp. His writings are convoluted and obscure if you are not used to such philosophical or linguistic gymnastics. Part of the problem in approaching Whitehead is that our language is really working against us. Ours in a noun-based language, in which things perform actions, which makes it frightfully difficult to describe a universe in which there are no things. In fact, there are only two languages known to human history that are verb-based languages, and actually suited to the job: Hebrew and Hopi.

Due to the fact that Whitehead was writing (and thinking!) in English, this presented him with a formidable problem. English is simply the wrong tool for the job. Consequently, to compensate for this, he had to forge a vocabulary to help him describe a reality for which the English language is simply ill-suited.

Nevertheless, we, too, are writing, reading (and most likely thinking) in English, and so Whitehead's vocabulary is the best tool at hand for the job. If there are no such things as things or beings, and every thing or being we perceive is actually an event, how do events relate to one another?

Whitehead said that events are nested inside larger events. For instance, a cell in my body is an event, that is nested within a larger event which is my kidney, which is nested within a larger event called John, which is nested within a larger event called California, which is nested within a larger event called North America, which is nested within a larger event called the Earth, which is nested within a larger event called the Milky Way Galaxy, which is nested within a larger event called the Universe, which is nested within a larger event we call "God." These nested fields of becoming Whitehead called *nexus*. Everything and everyone we know is involved in some nexus or another.

God is the largest event — and the largest nexus — we can conceive of, and is the One Event that is becoming. In fact this is very similar to the name that the Hebrew God gave to Moses from the burning bush: "I am what I am becoming." God then, for Whitehead is not above and beyond creation, is not separate from it, but is bound up with it, becoming as it is becoming, and thus is ever-changing and always evolving. And just as we have a visible body and an invisible mind, God is likewise evolving in visible and invisible planes.

God can be spoken of as being "bi-polar," not in a psychopathological way, but as having two co-existent poles, or ways of becoming, which we perceive as being transcendent on the one hand, and imminent on the other. It is tempting to speak of these as being analogous to body and mind, but these are things rather than processes, so they are of limited help as analogies. They are more like God's conscious (imminent) becoming and unconscious (transcendent) becoming.

Whitehead calls this imminent nature God's *consequent nature*. This is the evolving universe, which is always changing, always evolving, always growing, as we can easily see with our eyes, whether naked or aided by microscope or telescope. *This* transcendent nature—what Whitehead calls God's *primordial nature*—is harder to grasp. It is the repository of all potentiality, where all that has ever been is remembered, and all that may become is held in trust. In Jungian terms this is kind of like the collective unconscious. In Platonic terms, it is kind of like the World of Forms. This is the metaphorical "place" where every fear, every pain, every idea, every moment of every life is kept safe, and generously made available to all occasions at all times, unconsciously informing every event in the phenomenal universe, continually whispering, inspiring, informing, nudging.

God, in Whitehead's system, has what he calls an *initial aim* — a direction God wants the universe to move in; which is always toward greater complexity, greater diversity, greater creativity. In more traditional religious language, we might call this "God's will," but for Whitehead, it does not have an aura of judgment around it.

Lesser occasions (such as us) have complete free will in this system, however. We possess *subjective aim*, which can often be at odds with God's initial aim. And here is where the very real danger creeps into Whitehead's system. If we want to, we can thwart God's plans. For Whitehead's God is not omnipotent and does not possess ultimate power. This God has no power to intercede, no mechanism by which to alter history. God has the power only to suggest, to whisper, to inspire, but not the power to coerce or to suspend the laws of nature.

Whitehead's God cannot defy physics, cannot pluck falling planes out of the sky, cannot rescue a race bound for genocide. For God has, as St. Therese said, no hands on earth but ours, and cannot help if we will not listen. God can only, at best, scream. If we choose not to listen, then God is as helpless as the victims. This makes God the weakest of all occasions in a way, since God cannot directly act in the universe. And yet, the Divine, alone among all other occasions, has the power to suggest—to whisper—to every occasion in the universe simultaneously. Now, that is not absolute power, but it does mean that the divine has more power than anything else in the universe.

Such a system certainly solves the major philosophical dilemma of the impossible triangle. For Whitehead's system denies not just one point, but two. First, Whitehead's God is not all-good, and so is not perfect. Whitehead's God means well, but needs lesser occasions (like us) in order to develop morally. It is only in community that we learn to be more human than animal, and this is no less true for God. The record of our religious traditions can be seen as a school of moral development for Divinity as well as for humanity. Indeed, we have grown up together.

Second, as we have seen, God is not all-powerful in Whitehead's system. Since God can only suggest and not coerce, there are many evils wrought in "his" name that have been entirely beyond God's control. The Divine is also limited in another way: traditionally, we think of God as being outside of time. But in Whitehead's system, God is trapped in time. It is always now, and there is no miraculous "otherworld" against which it should be any other time. So the Divine is always in the now, and always becoming. The Divine does not know how this will all unfold. This means that God does not know if the project of the world is going to succeed or fail.

How does this model redeem God? Perhaps it doesn't, especially if the model is not viable for you. For myself, it is not perfect, but it is the best model I have come across to date. It leaves the fewest questions unanswered, and squares the best with contemporary science and with my own experience of the Divine. Whitehead's God is not the almighty judge, the god of wrath, rape, or genocide. Instead, this God is the "fellow sufferer who understands."

In a song I wrote not too long ago, Whitehead's God sings,

So if what you're looking for is a powerful God
who scatters his foes and bathes in their blood,
I'm afraid I'm not going to be much good to you.
But if what you need is somebody close by,
who suffers when you suffer,
and cries when you cry,
who cheers at your victories,
and holds you when you die,
then I'm there for you...
("The Defense," Mind Furniture, 2007)

If Whitehead's vision is true, then God is the most maligned "person" in history. God has had to sit back and listen to "his" good name be used to justify the most horrific actions. Although God has no doubt been whispering furiously against it, "he" has been ultimately unable to stop it. We have projected onto this hapless being, this (in many ways) helpless occasion, the sum total of our greed, bloodlust, and fear-driven murderousness. We have called good, "evil," and evil, "good." We have used the pretense of holiness to wreck unspeakable terrors, and blamed it on God. We have spun elaborate lies to implicate Divinity in our own sins, and to justify our own horrific behavior.

And yet, through it all, God has not abandoned us. Perhaps this is the true meaning of the crucifixion—not the payment of some cosmic debt, or to satisfy the bloodlust of the Father disguised as "justice"—but a snapshot of an immutable truth: although we spit on and torture "him," malign and slander "him," hate and berate "him," God remains in union with all flesh, fixed to the cross of the world until the end of time, all out of love for us—ignorant and violent creatures that we are.

There is not a story in this book that cannot be understood according to Whitehead's system. Most of these evils can be seen as devices of our own creation, projected onto God through myth and hymn to serve our own need for safety and power, or simply for political convenience. Perhaps some of them reveal God's true development as a moral being, learning to empathize and check "his" temper and other unruly emotions. Some stories were no doubt told just because humans needed someone to blame for things beyond their control, and God has been the ultimate scapegoat long before Jesus of Nazareth was handed that mantle.

Process Thought is not an easy way out as far as vindicating Divinity or explaining the problem of evil. It is, in fact, very messy. For you are left with a God shorn of superhuman powers who does not have the ability to intervene in human affairs (beyond the power of suggestion). You also must deal with a God who, although meaning well, is still sorting out right from wrong, and does so in collaboration with us in what is, in retrospect, a horrific and seemingly endless dance of trial and error. This is, in many ways, not a very attractive God. But if the only alternative is the Monster God—and logically, I believe that it is, either that or no God at all—then for my money, it is no contest.

What is Our Responsibility?

If Whitehead's model is close to describing objective reality, then we have a choice to make: do we assist God in the project of the universe, or do we resist the Divine effort? This is a question we must take seriously, because it really does makes a difference. In this system, the Divine is as dependent on us as we are on it. God can only evolve through interaction with lesser occasions, so the Divine needs the drama of the universe to play out in order to grow, to learn, to vision, to become.

So we can choose to help the Divine or not. We can be, in traditional terms, a sinner or a saint. But just what do those terms mean within this system? In Process thought the greatest virtue is creativity, and the greatest sin is doing the same old thing. To sin is to refuse to change, to grow, to experiment, to be creative. It is the refusal to evolve, to flower, to become more than you are.

To have virtue is to be quite the opposite: to have the courage to experiment, to grow, to make mistakes, to learn, to create combinations previously unthought of, to relish the unknown, to leap into it with trust and abandon.

Of course, that means that for optimal creativity and diversity, a balance between chaos and stability must be maintained, and according to Process Thought, the Divine is hard at work to maintain this balance within norms that can most encourage creativity, change, and diversity.

Now we know God's real weakness: the Divine is a novelty junkie. Novelty is the primary food of Whitehead's God, it is the outcome the Divine most urgently desires from every evolving occasion.

Unfortunately, we humans are afraid of change and frequently refuse to cooperate with the God's initial aim. On the other hand, if we choose to cooperate, the Divine's primordial nature is available to us at any time to inspire us. We can intentionally draw from this infinite repository of ideas, we have access to every thought that has ever been thought, and every combination that has ever been tried is there at our disposal if we will only be quiet enough to hear the Divine whisper.

If we can do that, we may be able to assist God in steering the project of the world toward a reality that eschews the horrors of the past, that envisions a way of being human—as well as a way of being Divine—that elicits more love and creativity than it does blood and terror. We must dream into the beings we most want to become.

We won't do this by ignoring the past, or sweeping it under the rug. The true God can handle our rage and other uncomfortable feelings, and indeed these must be part of the conversation if we are to enter into anything more than superficial relationship with the Divine. The Monster God must be part of the discussion, and a large part. We will avail ourselves nothing by ignoring this aspect of Divinity, excusing it, or even explaining it away. We must, in our prayer, acknowledge the elephant in the room.

Only then is real relationship—the thing the True God earnestly desires—possible. The glory of Whitehead's vision is that the True God needs this relationship as much as we do. Without our fulfillment, God has none, either. It is my prayer that this book will begin an honest conversation between readers and the True God, one that acknowledges all the darkness and pain, and that denies none of the ambiguity or complexity inherent in any intimate relationship.

It is also my hope that it will move readers to choose to assist God in the project of the world. There is still war and pain and hunger and hatred in the world, far too much. By confronting the false stories we tell ourselves, by uncovering the rationalizations and prejudices enshrined in our sacred mythmaking, I hope that we can move beyond such Divine slander and self-satisfied blasphemies to create a truly moral world where every event can be held as precious, worthwhile, and Divine.

We need to take responsibility for our concept of God, and our relationship to it. If our images of God are projections of our own worst traits, it is time we owned our projections. If our idea of God necessarily includes the qualities of omnipotence and all-beneficence, perhaps we are deluding ourselves and should rethink our ideas. If God truly is an unredeemable demon, perhaps it is time to get a new God.

Our internalized image of the Monster God and the many acolytes who serve "him" will do everything in their power to thwart such an eventuality. But, as the Gnostics divined, another God, a True God, whispers to us a different vision. Will we listen? It is not only God's redemption that depends upon this answer. It is ours, as well.

I call upon heaven and earth this day to bear witness
that I have set before you life and death,
blessings and curses.
Choose life
so that you and your descendants may live...

Deuteronomy 30:19

Notes

CHAPTER ONE

1 See Barnes, Michael H. *In the Presence of Mystery: An Introduction to the Story of Human Religiousness* (Mystic, CT: Twenty-Third Publications, 1984) for a more complete description of the stages of cultural and religious development.

2 Radin, Paul. *Primitive Religion* (New York: Dover, 1952), 54-5.

3 Radin, 261.

4 Knappert, Jan. *The Aquarian Guide to African Mythology* (London: The Aquarian Press/Harper Collins, 1990), 126.

5 Grimm, Jacob. *Teutonic Mythology* (New York: Dover, 1966), 20.

6 Brahmavaivarta Purana, quoted in O'Flaherty, Wendy Doniger. *The Origins of Evil in Hindu Mythology* (Berkeley: The University of California Press, 1976), 140.

7 Linga Purana, quoted in O'Flaherty, *Origins*, 140.

8 Jaiminiya Brahmana, quoted in O'Flaherty, *Origins*, 140.

9 O'Flaherty, *Origins*, 142.

10 *Ibid.*, 91.

11 O'Flaherty, Wendy Doniger. *Hindu Myths* (New York: Penguin Books, 1975), 36.

12 Taittiriya Samhita, quoted in O'Flaherty, *Origins*, 92.

13 Quoted in O'Flaherty, *Origins*, 66.

14 Deuteronomy 11:26-28.

CHAPTER TWO

1 Knappert, 83.

2 *Ibid.*

3   Radin, 244.
4   Dr. L. Benedict, quoted in Radin, 244-5.
5   Knappert, 125.
6   *Ibid.*, 81.
7   Kerényi, C. *The Gods of the Greeks* (London: Thames and Hudson, 1951), 106.
8   Macrone, Michael. *By Jove!* (New York: HarperCollins, 1992), 35-6.
9   Rosenberg, Donna. *World Myths* (Lincolnwood, IL: National Textbook Company, 1988), 178.
10 Grimm, 167-8.
11 Crim, Keith, ed. *The Perennial Dictionary of World Religions* (San Francisco: Harper & Row, 1981), 7.
12 Kramer, Samuel Noah, ed. *Mythologies of the Ancient World* (Chicago: Quadrangle Books, 1961), 450.
13 Bryant, Page. *The Aquarian Guide to Native American Mythology* (London: The Aquarian Press/Harper Collins, 1991), 140.
14 Smith, Homer W. *Man and His Gods* (New York: Grossett & Dunlap, 1952), 75-6.
15 Lloyd-Jones, Hugh. *The Justice of Zeus* (Berkeley: University of California Press, 1971), 3.
16 *Ibid.*, p. 16.
17 Knappert, 61.
18 Smith, 35.
19 *Ibid.*, 22.
20 *Ibid.*, 72-4.
21 Taittiriya Upanishad, III, 2 and 10, 6.
22 Daniélou, Alain. *Gods of Love and Ecstasy: The Traditions of Shiva and Dionysus* (Rochester: Inner Traditions International, Inc., 1984), 164.
23 O'Flaherty, Wendy Doniger. *Tales of Sex and Violence: Folklore, Sacrifice, and Danger in the Jaiminiy Brahmana* (Chicago: The University of Chicago Press, 1985), 57.
24 *Ibid.*, 58.

25   O'Flaherty, *Origins*, 86.

26   Satapatha Brahmana, 4.5.7.7.

27   Rodhe, Sten. *Deliver Us From Evil* (Lund, Copenhagen: Swedish Society for Missionary Research, 1946), 64-5, quoted in O'Flaherty, *Origins*, 171.

28   O'Flaherty, *Origins*, 170.

29   Daniélou, Alain. *The Myths and Gods of India* (Rochester: Inner Traditions International, Inc., 1985), 195.

30   Daniélou, *Shiva*, 83.

31   Daniélou, *Myths*, 47.

32   *Ibid.*, 48.

33   O'Flaherty, *Origins*, 171.

34   Hillebrandt, Alfred. *Vedic Mythology: Vols I & II* (Delhi: Motilal Banarsidass, 1891), 160.

35   Kinsley, David. *Hindu Goddesses: Visions of the Divine Feminine in the Hindu Religious Tradition* (Berkeley: The University of California Press, 1988), 36-7.

36   Ramanujan, A.K. *Speaking of Siva* (New York: Penguin Books, 1973), 71.

37   Daniélou, *Myths*, 219.

38   Kinsley, 158-9.

39   *Ibid.*, 152.

40   *Ibid.*, 144.

41   *Ibid.*, 139-40.

42   *Ibid.*, 100.

43   *Ibid.*, 96-7.

44   *Ibid.*, 100.

45   *Ibid.*, 118.

46   Daniélou, *Myths*, 271.

47   Kinsley, 116.

48   *Ibid.*, 118.

49   *Ibid.*, 119.

50   *Ibid.*, 128.

51   Daniélou, *Myths*, 138.

52 *Ibid.*, 283.

53 *Ibid.*, 168.

54 Georg Baudler. *God and Violence* (Springfield: Templegate, 1992), 67.

CHAPTER THREE

1   Campbell, Joseph. *Primitive Mythology* (New York: Viking Press, 1959), 275-6.

2   Knappert, 81.

3   *Ibid.*, 189.

4   *Ibid.*, 84.

5   Bryant, 75.

6   Knappert, 223.

7   *Ibid.*, 84.

8   Biallas, Leonard J. *Myths, Gods, Heroes, and Saviors* (Mystic: Twenty-Third Press, 1986), 88.

9   Macrone, 43.

10 *Ibid.*, 43

11 Lloyd-Jones, 33.

12 Macrone, 44-5.

13 *Ibid.*, 29-30.

14 Kramer, 247.

15 Barnes, Hazel E. *The Meddling Gods* (Lincoln: University of Nebraska Press, 1974), 104.

16 Lloyd-Jones, 63.

17 Macrone, 58.

18 *Ibid.*, 58-9.

19 Rosenberg, 7.

20 O'Flaherty, *Origins*, 67.

21 *Ibid.*, 174.

22 *Ibid.*, 181.

23 O'Flaherty, *Sex*, 51-2.

24 Kinsley, 104.

25 O'Flaherty, *Origins*, 176.

26 *Ibid.*, 188.

27 *Ibid.*, 186.

28 *Ibid.*, 188.

29 *Ibid.*, 60.

30 Ellwood, Gracia Fay. *Batter My Heart* (Wallingford: Pendle Hill Publications, 1988), p. 8.

31 2 Samuel 24:1ff.

32 Judah Goldin, ed. *The Living Talmud* (New York: New American Library, 1957), 142.

CHAPTER FOUR

1 Knappert, 24.

2 *Ibid.*, 142.

3 Smith, 30.

4 Bryant, 87.

5 Macrone, 84.

6 Kerényi, 175.

7 *Ibid.*, 113.

8 *Ibid.*, 253.

9 *Ibid.*, 114.

10 *Ibid.*, 106.

11 Rosen, 17.

12 O'Flaherty, *Myths*, 34-5.

13 Daniélou, 108.

14 O'Flaherty, *Myths*, 92-3.

15 Daniélou, *Gods*, 112.

16 *Ibid.*, 173.

17 O'Flaherty, *Myths*, 54.

18 Many thanks to Jewish scholar David Blumenthal for highlighting these passages in his book, *Facing the Abusing God* (Louisville: Westminster/John Knox Press, 1993).

19 I am indebted to www.evilbible.com for this and the following two examples.

20 Talmud, Abodah Zarah 36B-37A. I am endebted to the

www.answering-christianity.com website for bringing this example to my attention.

21 Ezekiel 16, NRSV.

22 Blumenthal, David R. *Facing the Abusing God* (Louisville: Westminster/John Knox Press, 1993), 240.

23 Barnstone, Willis and Marvin Meyer, eds. *The Gnostic Bible* (Boston: Shambhala, 2003), 159.

24 Layton, Bentley. *The Gnostic Scriptures* (New York: Doubeday, 1983), 71.

25 Harold Bloom, *The American Religion* (New York: Simon & Schuster, 1992).

26 Young, Brigham. *Journal of Discourses* 1:50-51.

27 This is based on a misreading of Sura 24: 2-14, originally intended to protect women—specifically *a* woman, Mohammad's wife, Aisha, who had been falsely accused of adultery.

28 From the Human Rights Watch website www.hrw.org.

29 Ibn Hisham. Al Rod Al Anf, Vol. 2, 182.

30 Sunaan Abu Dawud 112150.

31 Ayatollah Khomeini, Yahrirolvasyleh, Vol. 4 (Iran: Darol Elm, 1990)

CHAPTER FIVE

1 Rosenberg, 470 ff.

2 *Ibid.*, 459.

3 James A. Haught, *Holy Horrors* (New York: Prometheus Books, 1990), pps. 32-33.

4 *Ibid.*, 32.

5 Rosenberg, 22-26.

6 Daniélou, *Myths*, 196.

7 Mahabharata, Anusasana Parvan 45.313, quoted in Danielou, *Myths*, 201.

8 Haught, 34-35.

9 *Ibid.*, 43-47.

10 *Ibid.*, 49-52.

11 *Ibid.*, 43-52.

12 Christie-Murray, David. *A History of Heresy* (New York: Oxford, 1976), 108.

13 Haught, 42.

14 Frank Chalk and Kurt Jonassohn, *The History and Sociology of Genocide* (New Haven: Yale University Press, 1990), 249ff.

CHAPTER SIX

1 Wilson, Andrew. *World Scripture: A Comparative Anthology of Sacred Texts* (New York: Paragon House), 244.

2 Daniélou, *Myths*, 133-4.

3 Wilson, 255.

4 Rabbi Yoel Moshe Teitelbaum, Va-Yoel Mosheh and Al ha Ge'ulah ve-al ha-Temurah.

5 Harwood, William. *Mythology's Last Gods* (Buffalo: Prometheus Books, 1992), 46.

6 See John 3:36, Rom 1:18, Eph 5:6. Mackey, Virginia. *Punishment In the Scripture and Tradition of Judaism, Christianity, and Islam* (New York: National Interreligious Task Force on Criminal Justice, 1983), 36.

7 Matt 25:31-46, NRSV.

8 Mark 9:43-49, NRSV.

9 Rev 20:9-15, NRSV.

10 Harwood, 45.

11 Joyce, James. *Portrait of the Artist as a Young Man* (New York: B. W. Huebsch, 1916), 143-146 (page numbers refer to the 1993 Garland edition).

12 Toshihiko Izutsu *God and Man in the Koran* (Tokyo: Keio Institute of Cultural and Linguistic Studies, 1964), 234.

CHAPTER SEVEN

1 Morrish, 24.

2 Masani, Rustom. *Zoroastrianism: The Religion of the Good Life*

(New York: Collier Books, 1962), 65.

3   *Ibid.*, 23.
4   *Ibid.*, 24.
5   *Ibid.*, 21.
6   *Ibid.*, 18.
7   Harwood, 34.
8   Lacarriere, Jacques. *The Gnostics* (San Francisco: City Lights, 1989), 46–47.
9   Blumenthal, 33.
10 Lacarriere, 29.

CHAPTER EIGHT

1   Priestland, Gerald. *The Case Against God* (London: Collins, 1984), 141-142.
2   Fortune, Marie F. "The Transformation of Suffering: A Biblical and Theological Perspective" *in Christianity, Patriarchy, and Abuse* ed. by Joanne Carlson Brown and Carole R. Bohn (Cleveland, OH: Pilgrim Press, 1989), 140.
3   Blumenthal, 251.
4   Jung, C.G. *Answer to Job*, (New Jersey: Bollingen Publishing).
5   Blumenthal, 250.
6   Lacarriere, 25.
7   Priestland, quoting Jonothan Miller, 20.
8   Blumenthal, 43.
9   *Ibid.*, 42-43.
10 Baudler, 45.
11 Sontag, 46.
12 *Ibid.*, 135.
13 *Ibid.*, 136.
14 Blumenthal, 266.
15 *Ibid.*, 267.
16 *Ibid.*
17 Elizabeth Bettenhausen, "Forward" in *Christianity, Patriarchy, and Abuse.*